James G. Watt

...from the life of your father and grandfather

Stuff That Matters

...from the life of your father and grandfather

STUFF THAT MATTERS

by
James G. Watt

XULON PRESS

ACKNOWLEDGMENTS

My special thanks to Erin for spending some of her vacation applying comma rules to this and to Leilani for being my encouraging general editor. You attended to important stuff ... like leaving it imperfect enough so that I feel like I am really telling you these stories.

Tell us again...

"Dad, tell us the story about ... Our kids don't remember it." So I started writing down the stories about the incidents of my life that have impacted me, made a difference – that have value.

For Father's Day in 2005 I printed out the first few pages, slipped them in cover sheets, with the promise of more stuff to come, and sent the stories in nearly empty notebooks to you, all twelve of you: *Erin* and Terry (Joel, Kara, Ethan, Laura, Elliot and Trent) and *Eric* and Becky (Ian and Kiersti).

I want to leave you a legacy, not of goods or money, but of influence and of principles for life that have transferable value, the stuff that matters. It's now 2013 and this book is a gift for each of you.

Some of you reading this book are not directly related, but I hope my random presentation of short (some very short) stories from my life makes you feel as if you are family. Some of you will have heard a few of these in one form or other – or are the subject of them. I make no apology. Some of you were there when they happened and some of you never knew it mattered to me.

I want all you kids to know that great moments and valued experiences don't come from the complexities of life and sophisticated education, but from simple truths and day to day experiences – the ah-ha's of life. Or as your mother would say, the holy moments: the insightful times in our lives when we should say, *Selah,* that Hebrew word we find in the Bible, that means stop and pause and think on these things you have just read.

This book is about the *Selah* moments in my life plus a few other incidents, stories and fun times – stuff that matters.

TABLE OF CONTENTS

DO YOU UNDERSTAND?............................... 17
WHAT I LEARNED FROM THE PRESIDENTS 19
THE COMMON THREAD BETWEEN THE
     PRESIDENTS I KNEW 27
TWO STEPS WITH DAD 31
MY THEOLOGY 35
PLAIN TOMATO JUICE................................. 37
THE LAMB'S PASTURE 45
TRADITIONS.. 51
WALKING THE WALLS OF JERUSALEM 55
"I WILL DEFEND YOU"................................. 57
WALKING WITH ERIN.................................. 61
STANDING BEFORE A HIGHER COURT 63
IT IS NOT WHO YOU KNOW 65
EXPECTING A RESPONSE.............................. 69
GOD TURNED AWAY FROM ME....................... 79
PREPLANNED SPONTANEOUS ANSWERS 85
A MAN WHO KNOWS HIS POSITION............... 95
GOD IS OUR SOURCE 101
WILLING TO DISSENT 105
DO YOU KNOW JESUS? 107
THE PRIDE OF LIFE................................... 115

SURRENDERING TO ORTHODOXY 121
WORTH DOING POORLY! 127
ROMANCE - CUT FLOWERS AND GOING
  OUT TO EAT 131
DETERMINED TO FINISH STRONG 137
DIVERSITY, AMBIGUITY AND PARADOXES 141
IT'S WORTH SEEING, BUT IT'S NOT WORTH
  GOING TO SEE 145
HOW TO PICK A CHURCH 149
ASSUME THE PERSON AGREES WITH YOU 151
SUCCESS AND SIGNIFICANCE 153
JAMES WATT'S GOD 157
NO MORE BLACK CHICKENS 159
MARRIAGE COUNSELING 167
RIYADH 171
THE WAILING WALL OF JERUSALEM 175
BE LED NOT PUSHED 179
THE SMARTEST KID IN THE DUMB CLASS 181
YOU ARE NOT ALONE 185
PRESENTING MY WORLDVIEW 189
JOHNNY COOPER 193
MY DAD WAS FOR ME 201
SISTER SIZEMORE 203
FRIENDS OF ISRAEL 207
THE JERICHO MARCH 211
DO NOT ACCELERATE THE PLANS OF GOD 215
LEARNING FROM THE LEFT 223
THE SEVENTH MENTIONING 229
REAGAN'S KINDNESS 233
ENCOURAGING OTHERS 241
THE MONDAY MORNING GROUP 243

TABLE OF CONTENTS

WHO RULED THE ROOST? 247

FRIENDSHIP 249

THE UMBRELLA STORY 253

FRIENDS AND ENEMIES 261

ADVERSITY AND BLESSING 269

COURAGE.. 275

I SAVED THE BEST TILL LAST...................... 279

BE THERE!... 285

APPENDIX: 287

LET REAGAN BE REAGAN........................... 289

" ... IN A TOWN NEAR-BY"........................... 295

REAGAN'S RADIO ADDRESS........................ 311

PHOTO AND DOCUMENT CREDITS................ 317

DEDICATION

Dedicated to your mother and grandmother:
Leilani
A woman who knows God.
A role model on living a life for Christ.
A lady who has given and given - to all of us;
A faithful wife who has carried my
stretcher on many occasions and has been
my closest friend since the 8th grade.

James Watt - Jr. High picture

Leilani Bomgardner - Jr. High picture

DO YOU UNDERSTAND?

The following short stories from the last fifty years reveal some answers to a challenging question. The question was presented on a spring day in the early 1960s at a Capitol Hill bus stop in Washington, DC. I stood with a collection of people waiting for a bus. I was on my way home to your mother, a marvelous, bright, active, attractive, spiritual wife and to the two of you magnificent, healthy little kids (a king's family: a girl, Erin and a boy, Eric). Being right out of law school, I had the perfect job as Legislative Assistant and Counsel to Wyoming's Republican United States Senator. Brief case in hand, satisfaction and confidence radiating.

An older man, tall and heavy, dressed in clean bib-overalls, looked me in the eye and said, **"Young man, do you understand what you know?"**

Selah.

WHAT I LEARNED FROM
THE PRESIDENTS

This topic is one that I have used as an outline for many of the speeches I have given around the country, paid and unpaid. I have used the topic at Elliot's high school graduation, at many Rotary and Lions clubs, and at Chamber of Commerce banquets, etc. Usually I tie this outline to the story that follows under the chapter, "The Common Thread Between the Presidents I Knew."

President Dwight D. Eisenhower (1953-1961):

When I was in high school in Wyoming, I won a trip to Washington, DC. (I had been elected Governor of Boy's State and selected to go to Boy's Nation). I was thrilled because I, along with another ninety-nine Boy's Nation members, would go to the White House and meet President Eisenhower, my hero. In preparation for the trip, my father sat me down and explained to me that the boys from the East

19

Coast states would act as if they were superior to the boys from the West. "But remember, James, every man puts his pants on one leg at a time."

I was thrilled to be in the Rose Garden as we waited for the President to come out of the Oval Office. With anticipation I craned my neck to catch the first glimpse of the President. As I saw him come out of the door, my first thought was, "Even the President of the United States puts his pants on one leg at a time." I knew at that moment: **All men are created equal.**

President John Kennedy/President Lyndon Johnson (1961-1969):

After graduating from the University of Wyoming law school, I went to Washington, DC, with Milward Simpson the then United States Senator from Wyoming. He opposed President Kennedy with every ounce of his being. I wrote for him a series of blistering speeches against the Kennedy/Johnson Administration. Because of the assassination of President Kennedy, the hostile speeches were soon focused on President Johnson as he initiated the legislative program for his Great Society.

After his 1964 election, the President and Mrs. Johnson invited Senator and Mrs. Simpson to a private dinner party in their upstairs home in the White House. Two days later a beautiful portrait photograph (in color, a new thing in those days) came to the office, autographed by the President with a kind remark about my senator. It was a fine picture of the President and the Senator with their wives.

As the Senator studied the portrait, he turned to me and said, "I won't be making any more hostile speeches about President Johnson." I learned that some biblical principles are also applicable to politics: **It is hard to criticize one with whom you have shared a meal**.

President Richard M. Nixon (1969-1974):

I headed up a major bureau in the Department of the Interior for President Nixon. I was given charge of preparing an important study for the President to submit to the Congress. I finished the report on time and under budget and sent it over to the White House for the signature of the President. The report kept getting shifted from one office to another and time was running out. I asked my boss, the then Secretary of the Interior, Walter Hickel, if he would get the President to sign the study at the next meeting they had. He assured me that he would. I awaited his return with expectation. When he returned, Secretary Hickel told me that he had failed to get the signature because the meeting was with men of such a high rank, no one knew how to get things done. It became obvious: **Just because you hold a big title, and may know what you want to do, does not mean that you know how to do it.**

President Gerald R. Ford (1974-1977):

President Ford appointed me to a fixed, five-year term on the quasi-judicial Federal Power Commission. The appointment required approval by the Democrat-controlled Senate. I was found qualified for the appointment (and the Senate concurred) because I knew absolutely nothing about the subject or the industries to be regulated by the Commission to which I was appointed. It was reassuring to know: **You do not need to know everything about a subject before you are deemed qualified to tackle the job or the assignment**.

President Jimmy Carter (1977-1981):

Since President Ford had sent me to the Federal Power Commission for a fixed term, it made no difference to me employment-wise, who won the 1976 presidential election. My employment was secure. In fact I was doing so well, I had been promoted to serve as Vice

Chairman of the FPC. After President Carter's election, however, the Congress decided to abolish the Federal Power Commission and my job. I was again reminded: **There are no guarantees in life.**

President Ronald W. Reagan (1981-1989):

With President Reagan's election, I was selected to be the Secretary of the Interior. In August of that first year, Reagan's Chief of Staff, Jim Baker, returned to Washington, DC, from an August fishing trip with our then Wyoming Congressman, Dick Cheney. Baker had learned about a huge controversy I was experiencing because of an application to drill for oil in the environmentally sensitive Jackson Hole area. Baker called and asked me what I was going to do about it. I told him I was going to have to deny the drilling application because of the political opposition. He said I must speak to the President about it. (Just a few days earlier my long time fraternity friend and later Governor, Mike Sullivan, had called and warned me about potential death threats because of the controversy. I quickly notified our security people and was surprised to learn that they were well aware of the threats and had taken 'appropriate' action.)

I did not want to meet with the President.

I was embarrassed that I had drawn so much negative press. Press stories echoing the liberal and environmental communities' opposition to our energy programs. Over my objections, Baker scheduled a fifteen minute meeting with the President for the next morning.

After a brief presentation of the problem, President Reagan spoke directly to me in his calm manner. I cannot tell you what he said, but I can tell you what I heard. "Jim, we were elected to do what is right for the country. If you do not issue the drilling permit, who will? If you do not drill there, where will you drill for oil?"

As the President was speaking to me, I had a flash-back and saw my father and mother saying to me, "James, you do what is right because it is right!"

Because Reagan was giving me a back-bone, I proceeded to present to him the host of environmental problems I was confronting at the Department of the Interior. He never flinched with the fear of hostile opposition. Forty-five minutes later, I left his Oval Office with a renewed determination to serve him and our country without fear of the personal abuse that I knew would come.

From that time on, President Reagan was faithful to communicate (directly and indi-rectly) words of encouragement whenever a particularly nasty newspaper article would appear.

In Reagan I saw the personification of the principle**: Do what is right without regard to the press or the public opinion of the moment.** As my folks taught, "Do what is right because it is right."

THE COMMON THREAD BETWEEN THE PRESIDENTS I KNEW

I was asked to speak to a junior high school History class that was studying the presidents of the United States. My assignment was to tell about the presidents I had known. I thought it would be instructive to read the text book the students were using. I was surprised that the History book only gave two or three sentences about each of the presidents. Just a couple of column inches to each. After getting over the shock of such brevity, I came to understand why an historian could be so brief – what really does matter in a person's life? I was intrigued with what the author chose to tell about the men with whom I had worked.

As I shared this story with Rotary Clubs, college classes, church groups, and others, I have involved the audiences in listing what they thought was important from an historian's point of view. There has never been any deviation in what people list as the important historical points they would write in two or three column inches to describe the years of service of these presidents of the United States.

President Nixon: Opening up China, Watergate, and his resignation. Getting out of Viet Nam.

President Ford: Pardoning (forgiving) Nixon and stumbling on stairs.

President Carter: (always with difficulty – but finally) The Camp David Accord and the malaise of our time.

President Reagan: Restoring the pride in America, rebuilding our Armed Forces, and defeating the atheistic forces of communism.

President George H.W. Bush: "Read my lips: No new taxes" and the Persian Gulf War.

President Clinton: Monica Lewinski, impeached, and the endless scandals. (I always made the point that I never actually knew Clinton; and they always laughed with understanding.)

On reviewing the comments in the History text book, I realized there was a common thread ~~~ running through all of the historical accounts of the several presidents I knew: it was their moral stand.

Nixon lied. ~~~ Ford forgave. ~~~ Carter helped Israel obtain peace with Egypt. ~~~ Reagan stood against the atheistic forces of communism. ~~~ Bush did not keep his promise of 'no new taxes'. ~~~ Clinton was impeached for lying.

From an historical perspective, what I learned from the presidents is that **the moral positions we take, good and bad, are the ones for which we are judged and remembered**. The other activities of life, no matter how important they may seem at the time, have no lasting consequence or value in light of history or eternity. Our financial status, our sports ability, our good looks, or popularity - nothing matters in the long term but our righteous or unrighteous conduct.

My father William G. Watt with me - 1943

TWO STEPS WITH DAD

My dad was a small-town lawyer in Lusk, Wyoming - an oil and ranch town with between fifteen hundred and two thousand people. We lived four or five blocks from the downtown business section and across the street from the grade school.

As a little boy, I was proud to walk with my dad as he went to work in the morning and after lunch. I was not allowed to cross the streets by myself, so I could only walk with Dad for one block – just to the 'church corner,' the Congregational Church where we attended.

Dad was a good father. A well-educated man: moral, honest, and respected. He was not an athlete, but he liked sports. He was not a good businessman – never making more than just a bare living. He was committed to Republican politics. The name Franklin Delano Roosevelt was a bad word in our house.

He was an excellent debater and public speaker. A good preacher – he studied the Bible often. I liked being with my dad. I listened to him talk with the grown-ups. I learned a lot listening to those conversations – conversations about people, the law, politics, sports, and government. He talked about ideas and concepts. Even though he did not make small talk with people, he had a keen sense of humor and a dry wit.

I vividly remember walking to work with my dad. On one of those days when I was probably about six years old, I said, "Dad, the kids say you should not step on a crack in the sidewalk because it'll break your mother's back."

Holding my hand as we walked he said, "Oh, I don't think so."

Looking up at him, I insisted "Yeah Dad, the kids say so. I always count the steps. Two steps in each square and I never step on a crack."

Silence.

"Dad, do you count the steps you take in each square?"

As our eyes met, "No, I don't count my steps. When you get older you will have more important things to think about than counting steps."

I didn't think that day would ever come; but right then it didn't make any difference. My dad loved me and let me walk to work with him, hand in hand.

Dad was right. Careers and great respon-sibilities have come my way so I didn't always focus on the sidewalk. I have had many more important things to think about. Even so, now as I take my daily walk some sixty or seventy plus years later, I sometimes say with a smile, "Yeah Dad, I still count my steps, avoiding the cracks and taking two steps to a square," **remembering time with my dad is what was important.**

MY THEOLOGY

After finishing our discussions at the early breakfast Bible study at the Snow King Resort, our group, The Old Wine in Old Wineskins, entered the men's room where there were three cowboys talking loudly.

One of them said forcefully, **"You tell them that I am a man of the highest moral character,"** and then in a smaller voice, **"subject to instant collapse."**

The room exploded with laughter.

I realized that statement summarized my theology. It explains why I need a Savior and the counsel and guidance of the Holy Spirit.

PLAIN TOMATO JUICE

I could not have been happier, or more excited after the election of 1962, to be named the Legislative Assistant and Legal Counsel to the newly elected United States Senator from Wyoming, Milward L. Simpson.

Right after graduating from the University of Wyoming's College of Law and taking the Wyoming Bar Examination, I had joined the campaign of Governor Simpson.

He won the November election and your mother and I, with you two little kids, headed directly to Washington, DC, to set up house. Every day was exciting for me. It was a thrill for this Wyoming country kid to go to work in the nation's capitol.

Early in 1963 the Senator asked me to escort the president of the University of Wyoming to a meeting in the Pentagon. I had never been to the Pentagon and was thrilled to go. In addition, I was getting to take the esteemed and honored president of my university to a meeting with the Chairman of the

Joint Chiefs of Staff, Curtis E. LeMay. General LeMay was a five-star general and a hero of World War II. He had been commander of the airplanes that dropped atomic bombs in Japan.

I can not overstate the excitement and thrill I experienced just to sit in that room with nearly fifty people - university presidents and military officials. General LeMay was presiding but he was being staffed by three-star generals and a host of other uniformed officers. I had never seen so many generals.

After a couple of hours, General LeMay explained that because the meeting had lasted longer than expected, he had asked the Secretary of the Air Force if we could have lunch in the Secretary's formal dining room. We were to be the General's guests!

I was impressed with the power and the grandeur of the Pentagon. I walked into the Secretary's dining room gawking at the beauty of the chandeliers, the ornate ceilings, and polished wood. My eye was drawn to groupings of men - decorated generals with stars on their shoulders and ribbons on their chests, and the university presidents, in dark blue business suits. But suddenly shock overwhelmed me! I recognized that waiters, Filipino navy personnel, were taking cocktail orders and I was instantly paralyzed with fear.

I had grown up in a home where beer and liquor were not served. As a high school student, I would never do anything that might bring shame to the family name. It would have been disgraceful for a member of our family under the age of twenty-one to be caught drinking.

When I went to college and joined a fraternity, I went to the beer busts. No one made an issue of my not drinking, so I didn't. When I went to law school, I presumed that I would drink because the reputation was "all those students boozed it up." I went to their beer busts and again no one made an issue of whether I drank or not. No one really cared. So I never did. I never learned to drink.

I did know however, that when in Washington, I would have to learn to drink because so much of the business – at least in the movies - was done over cocktails. It was my intention to learn to drink and fit into the social scene in Washington, 'to get along by going along'. Since this Pentagon meeting came about early on and unexpectedly, I had not yet learned the social graces required to get along in Washington. What was I to do?

The short Filipino in his navy uniform came to the small cluster of military brass where I was standing. He turned to me first and asked what I wanted. I was embarrassed. I did not know what to say. What was socially proper in the Pentagon? At lunch? In the dining room of the Secretary of the Air Force? I was by far the youngest one in the room, the least experienced, the country kid from Wyoming. What was I to do? I was humiliated at my inexperience and lack of confidence and he asked me the second time. I leaned over and quietly said, "Plain tomato juice, please."

In a loud voice he repeated, "Plain tomato juice?" With a red face and the desire to crawl through the cracks in the floor, I leaned down and quietly said, "Yes."

The several Filipino waiters walked up a small ramp and through swinging doors to fill their orders. I visualized my waiter yelling from that ramp at the top of his lungs, "Who ordered the plain tomato juice?" I moved over near the ramp. Tension in my being was at an all-time peak, ready to stop that waiter as he came out of the kitchen with my tomato juice, before he could yell out THE question.

Sweat broke out all over my body. I was determined not to be embarrassed further. I was not going to be belittled by this waiter in front of significant people.

Again and again I heard the swinging doors, watched the waiters come out with trays full of cocktails, but not one glass of tomato juice. I knew almost everyone had been served. Was he going to wait until the very last and then yell, "Who ordered the plain tomato juice?"

Just then I felt a touch on my shoulder and turned to see the outstretched hand of a man with several stars on his shoulders. I shook his hand. As I did, I heard the door swing open behind me and a voice about eighteen inches inches from my ear yell out, "Who ordered the plain tomato juice?"

With embarrassment, shame, and a desire to dissolve into the floor, I raised my hand as I turned to the waiter on the ramp and said with a muted voice, "I did."

When I reached to take my glass, I saw three glasses of tomato juice on his tray. As I took my glass I heard two strong voices coming right at me. Quickly I turned and saw reaching around me to get the other two glasses of tomato juice Duke Humphrey, President of the University of Wyoming and Curtis E. LeMay, the five-star General of the Air Force and Chairman of the Joint Chiefs of Staff for President Kennedy.

I squared my shoulders, smiled at my co-tomato juice drinkers, and observed that others in the room had ducked their heads. They stood with cocktails in their hands at a working luncheon in the Pentagon with the most powerful man in the United States military - and he was drinking plain tomato juice. As was I.

From that moment forward, I never had a hesitation or embarrassment in any social setting in Washington or elsewhere. I never bothered to learn how to order or drink cock-tails or beer. **I never needed to do so.**

Still today, when asked, I simply smile and say, "Plain tomato juice, please."

My pet lamb

THE LAMB'S PASTURE

When you kids were four and six, we bought a house in Camp Springs, Maryland, a suburb of Washington, DC. It was next to Mr. O'Bannon's farm where he had bantam chickens roosting in the trees and horses grazing his several acres. We had a skinny lot, an acre, that dropped off to a little stream below.

I wanted to have sheep in our backyard. In particular I wanted you kids to have the opportunity to bottle feed a hungry little lamb as I had done when I was a small boy. Much to my disappointment, however, none of you (your mother included) ever warmed to the idea. Finally I decided I would get a lamb and teach you kids about rural America where people raise their own food.

I drove down into Southern Maryland to a livestock auction barn, bought a three week old lamb, and brought it home in the back seat of our car. I hustled around buying bottles and formula and then fixing up a pen to keep the dogs out and the lamb in. I fed the lamb and tried to comfort the scared little animal. Finally, much later that first evening, I went upstairs to bed.

As I lay on the bed, I could hear the bleating of the lamb, lost in its strange surroundings. With each different sound, I sprang from the bed to the window to see if the lamb was still in the pen and safe. When dogs came from all over yelping, fighting, and barking, I raced down the stairs and out of the house to chase them away. The defenseless, wooly lamb didn't even recognize danger. I returned upstairs to bed and lay as a nervous and stiff man, ready to go forth in the defense of the innocent sheep.

As the clock ticked on, my body became aware of the need for sleep that it wasn't going to get because of my intense anguish for a frightened lamb. I decided that as soon as the sun came up, I would return the lamb to the livestock auction barn. It was not fair for me, my job, or my family to suffer such concern, nervousness, and lack of sleep, all because of a dumb lamb. Just as I made the determined decision to get rid of the sheep, the Lord spoke to my innermost being and said, "No, you will learn many lessons from this lamb. I will teach you what it means to be a sheep and what it means to be a shepherd."

Not understanding how I could learn anything from such a dumb critter, I continued
through the night to watch over my new
charge. After many more trips to the window
to shine a light down on the lonely, bleating
lamb, I decided to get the lamb, put it in the
dog's house, and take it into the garage where
it would be safe from all the dangers of that
dark night. As I carried the young lamb into
the protective shelter, the Lord spoke to my
soul and said, "The concern you have for this
lamb is similar to the concern and love I have
for you."

The Lord abegan to bring to mind some of
the parallels between the lamb and me as a
sheep and between myself and the Lord as a
shepherd.

To that lamb I was the provider, protector,
savior, master and keeper. During the dark
night the lamb did not recognize, appreciate,
thank, or acknowledge me. In fact it ran every
time I came to take care of it. Not until several
days had passed did the lamb begin to recognize the voice of its shepherd and accept the
provision, protection, and safety I offered it.

Sheep are defenseless, stupid followers
that need guidance and protection. Whenever
I looked down with love at this dumb, little,
needy lamb, I realized that is how God probably saw me. I, too, am a 'sheep' following my
Shepherd.

Still wanting you kids to be involved, I explained that I was naming the lamb Mutt for mutton (the meat of sheep) in that sheep had two purposes: to provide wool to wear and meat to eat. And further, I explained that in the fall we would have the lamb butchered. Neither of you seemed to register any interest or concern about the name or the purposed fate of this little lamb.

After a few weeks I bought sheeptight fencing and built a bigger pasture for my growing Mutt. It was a delight to look out the window and see the lamb grazing in the green pastures. I felt I was providing a real experience for you two kids.

One evening as I came driving home from work, I noticed a bunch of you youngsters racing and darting across the street and through the neighborhood. As I got a better view, I saw that you and your friends were running after several dogs. And then I saw the dogs were chasing my lamb. I slammed on the brakes, bailed from the car, and ran as fast as I could to catch Mutt, my lamb. Yes, by now it was my lamb.

My pet lamb had escaped beyond the boundaries I had built and was free from the constraints of the fenced, rolling green pastures. I had provided all any sheep should want, yet my lamb was on the other side of the fence where there was no safety. Outside the boundary, Mutt was free to go wherever he wanted; but unknowingly he had subjected himself to dangers of the hungry dogs, speeding cars, screaming kids, and the vastness of the unknown.

My lamb had no idea how to get back home. It was not until I scooped the lamb up in my arms and returned him to his green pastures that he had rest from the exhaustion of being chased. As his shepherd, I was the one who understood that my lamb needed the safety that comes from freedom within limitations.

I learned that I should accept the boundaries (limitations) the Lord has set for me because there is no safety in unbridled, unrestricted freedom.

I am compelled to tell this story because I do not believe either of you two kids, Erin or Eric, ever really identified with my pet lamb, Mutt. When it started turning cold in the fall months and it was time to butcher Mutt, none of you seemed to care. So all by myself I loaded up Mutt and drove some considerable miles to give my pet lamb to a petting zoo.

Selah.

TRADITIONS

I never thought it important to celebrate or even note birthdays, anniversaries, or special days. Live for the future not the past was my claim!

I have been wrong. I learned my lesson in an interesting way.

A White House secretary called and said I was to meet President Reagan at the Lincoln Memorial for a wreath laying ceremony on February 12, President Lincoln's birthday.

"Why me?" I whined. I had important work to do. A lot of people were depending upon me. I needed to get things done so others could do their work. Huge investments would be made based upon my decisions, etc. But, I was told – no, ordered - by Kitty (my wonderful and faithful secretary), "You are head of the National Park Service and the Lincoln Memorial is a part of the Park system. The President is visiting your facility." And then she added, "The President wants you there." The last sentence was compelling.

One never keeps the President waiting. I went early to the Lincoln Memorial on a blustery cold, humid, windy day. It seemed foolish for the President to risk his health for such an event. It was so bitterly cold the wind cut through to my bones. Only the White House press corp, three National Park rangers, and my driver and I were waiting for the President at the Memorial. I complained of the cold every moment of the wait.

"Mr. President," I greeted him as he stepped out of his car. I escorted him up the marble stairs, as I had been instructed by the National Park Rangers. He placed a wreath at the foot of the Lincoln statue. The cameras were clicking and the TV cameras rolling.

I noticed the whole mood had changed when Reagan stepped out of the limousine. He brought dignity and respect to that cold marble memorial. His presence radiated a reverence, not for himself but for Lincoln. A spirit of gratitude for Lincoln's legacy was manifested by Reagan. With this ability – was he acting or was it genuine or did it matter? – he personally demonstrated that what Lincoln represented was important for today.

The pomp and circumstance that Reagan brought to Washington was hungered for by the American people having survived the Carter years. Reagan showed that same respect and reverence for tradition as he toured America and the world. Whether it was in Ames, Iowa or Montgomery, Alabama; at the Berlin Wall or the fortieth anniversary of Normandy, Reagan's presence told us that we were standing on the shoulders of those who had gone before us and we were thankful for them.

I was very much aware that the biting cold wind had become insignificant with the awesome respect and admiration for Lincoln that Reagan brought. My mind shifted to my own life. Could I show honor and respect for others as he had done on Lincoln's birthday? As I thought about it I realized that the holidays – Christmas, Easter, Thanksgiving, Veteran's Day, etc., should be made significant and special. There is a purpose for which they are designated as important.

I should honor your mother on our anniversary, you kids on your birthdays, friends and grandchildren on special days. And especially the Lord, as directed in the fourth of the Ten Commandments. **I should affirm and honor friends and family, and those who have walked before me, on whose shoulders I stand.**

Traditions can be very important in our lives, it can change a bitter cold day into a wonderful warm one.

WALKING THE WALLS
OF JERUSALEM

When my grandson, Ethan, was eighteen, I took him with a group of ten others on a church-sponsored guided tour of Israel. It was a rich time in my life and in Ethan's.

We visited all the tourist sights and sacred biblical locations possible. After stopping at the umpteenth pile of rocks (which at one time had been something special) I said to my friend Ed, "I've lost something." Eager himself to get away from the pile of rocks, he quickly came to my side and asked if he could help me find it. I told him that I did not think he could help: "I had lost interest." I never found it at any of the other piles of rock.

One morning the guide led our group on a walk along the top of the wall protecting the Old City of Jerusalem. As we walked high above the Old City, I quietly thanked the Lord for the privilege of walking where He had walked.

The Voice of the Living God said, **"It is better to walk with me now, than to have walked where I walked."**

Selah!

"I WILL DEFEND YOU"

In Reagan's 1980 campaign, he promised massive change in the way the government managed its natural resources. He declared himself to be a "Sagebrush Rebel." Governor Reagan was subjected to a brutal attack from the liberal environmental groups during the campaign and with an even greater intensity after he won the election.

We were living in Denver when I was selected and recommended by five United States senators to be Reagan's man at the Department of the Interior. Within the moment my name was made public as the President-elect's man, the attack shifted to me. We were not too concerned because we believed the facts were on Reagan's side and that I could present them in an understandable way.

In presenting myself to the public and discussing the natural resource issues, I was very open about my Christian faith and life. My Denver Assemblies of God pastor was very proud of me and kept giving my pentecostal testimony of praying in tongues.

Your mother and I were shocked to find the Washington press corps was not trustworthy. They were not concerned with facts about the natural resources or me and our family. The press corps was faithful to honestly report what some of the selfish interest groups were *charging and claiming* about Reagan, about me, and about my Christian faith, but they were not concerned whether or not the charges were true.

The liberal environmental groups raised tens of millions of dollars by their wild charges. Had there been any truth to what they said, I would also have chanted, "Dump Watt." And opposed those weird and warped religious views. But truth and reality were not guiding factors with those liberal groups.

My usual morning routine was to read the Bible, get dressed, eat, and leave in my chauffeur-driven car at 7:30 A.M. for a five minute drive to the office at the Department of the Interior. But in June of 1981 I also glanced at the morning *Washington Post*. There was a vile, hideous Herblock cartoon attacking me and also demeaning the Christian faith and all who might adhere to it. I was sickened beyond measure.

I had been withstanding attacks on my personality style and my life because I knew

I was doing what the President wanted, and what the Republican members of Congress supported. But this attack was not just about me. Although it was aimed at my very core, the cartoon also attacked all who shared the Christian faith. I pled with the Lord to rescue me and to get me out of this whole thing. Deliver me. Let me go.

With a heavy heart and feeling defeated, I reached for my Living Bible. It was open and I started reading at verse one of Psalm 62, "I stand silently before the Lord waiting for Him to rescue me ... " (TLB).

I was thrilled. I was going to be rescued. Suddenly a holy moment came upon me and God said to my heart, "I will not rescue you, but I will defend you."

Instantly I was filled with energy and was given a determination of steel. Your mother remembers that I came down the stairs after reading the Bible and hearing from God, picked her up, swung her around and said, "Hang on, Honey! It's going to get worse!"

I moved forward in the battle for America with a renewed intensity.

God was going to defend me.

Selah.

With Erin, age 6

WALKING WITH ERIN

When Erin was about six years old, she was invited to a birthday party by a neighborhood friend. I told her that I would walk her to the Saturday afternoon party. "No!" was her response. And that was that. She felt it would be embarrassing to be walked to the party. She was adamant. At six years of age she knew she could walk by herself and take care of herself. There was no room for compromise with that little head-strong girl.

So I walked across the street from her. I was there to watch over her and to help her, if need be. She was within my arc of protection.

But in her mind, she was not with me. She knew that and I knew that.

Yet I knew I was with her.

As I have reflected back on that vivid pictorial memory, **I realize I frequently have refused to walk with God,** even though He is walking with me. How often I have said in effect, "God, I can handle it from here." Rejecting His presence; rejecting the relationship. Oh, He is there 'walking across the street from me.' He is with me, but I am not with Him.

Forgive me Lord.

Selah !

STANDING BEFORE A
HIGHER COURT

As a young lawyer, I was privileged to go before the Supreme Court of the United States of America. I was counseled by others that it would be an awesome experience. I was told that many young lawyers had actually fainted as they stood before the Justices, the highest court of the land; others became speechless. I was also nervous and fearful of what might happen as I climbed the long, long stairway, entered the building, and found my way to the courtroom.

All of a sudden the Marshall of the Court sang out, "... All persons having business before the Honorable, the Supreme Court of the United States, are admonished to draw near and give their attention, for the Court is now sitting. God save the United States and this honorable Court."

Instantly, we all stood in awesome respect as the nine black-robed Justices moved to their chairs. Then we took our seats and the session of the Court began. Soon I heard the Chief Justice Earl Warren (Yes, I am that old!) call out, "Mr. Watt do you have business to present to the Court?"

I quickly moved to the podium and looked far up at the distinguished and powerful Justices seated behind the elevated bench of the Court. It was a quiet moment. I was the only one standing in the courtroom as the Justices looked down at me.

I felt alone.

I was alone.

Before I could say a word, I heard the voice of the Holy Spirit speak to my heart: "Some day you will stand before a higher Tribunal and you will be asked, 'Do you have business to present?'"

In fact each of us will stand alone - all by ourselves before God, the highest Tribunal - and **we will be judged for what we have done, both good and bad.**

Selah.

(P.S. The Court granted my motion. And I found confirmation of the words spoken to my heart in 2 Corinthians 5:10).

IT IS NOT WHO YOU KNOW

As a young man I fell into the trap of thinking that it was 'who you know' that was important. My friends would frequently tell me that they did not get a certain job because so and so knew the big boss and therefore got the job they had wanted. But I started noticing that opportunities were coming to me from people I did not know. Opportunities were coming because of who knew me and how I was known.

When Governor Reagan was elected, I had not been involved in the presidential campaign, nor did I know anybody who was. At that time, I was President of the Mountain States Legal Foundation and reported to our chairman, Joe Coors, who was well connected with the Reagan's. After the election Joe returned from a Washington meeting and told me that my name had come up as a possible member of the administration. And then he said, "I told them you were too young." I was flattered that my name had been mentioned, but I had no desire or dream of going to Washington, DC, in any capacity.

Our friend and former Senator from Wyoming, Cliff Hansen, was selected by the President-elect to be the new Secretary of the Department of the Interior. Your mother and I put the newspaper clipping on our refrigerator and prayed for Cliff.

He then determined that for family reasons he could not take the appointment. Governor Reagan asked five Western senators to get a candidate. I was told later that it was Senator McClure of Idaho who recommended they consider "this young man from Colorado who runs the Mountain States Legal Foundation." Several of the senators had heard about me and the work I was doing at the Foundation. I had never met four of the five. The fifth was Senator Al Simpson, son of Senator Milward Simpson, for whom I had worked. Al jumped on the suggestion and I was brought back to the Capitol for an interview with senators I had never known.

As I reflect back on my career, I can see that all my career planning and all my efforts to know the right people has been for naught. I never got a job, or a promotion, or an appointment because of who I knew.

My career was advanced because of who knew me - my character and my reputation for getting things done.

EXPECTING A RESPONSE

In several of these chapters I have told of the experiences I had around my speaking opportunities. All my professional years required that I speak in public forums. I was a good public speaker. Because I do not read well, I had to work hard preparing and memorizing the right phrases, in the right format, and with the right timing.

Your mother likes to tell the story of when we took you two kids with us to Colorado Springs so that you could hear me make an appeal to a large, important audience for funding of the Mountain States Legal Foundation. At the end of my presentation you, Erin, stood up looking for your purse and told your mother, "We have to help Dad. This is an important cause."

My speaking style did reach out and touch a person's heart or soul. That is why I was so popular on the speaking tours and at the same time why I drew such hostility.

At the second anniversary of Reagan's inauguration, the President asked all his political appointees to come to Constitution Hall which officially seats over three thousand seven hundred people. The place was filled and many were obliged to stand. I invited your mother to attend. Secretary of State, George Schultz, was to give a short presentation on our foreign accomplishments and I was asked to speak on domestic matters.

This would be the first time I had an opportunity to speak to a crowd with the whole Cabinet seated on the stage, and just prior to the Vice President and President. I worked hard in preparing my outline for this presentation, knowing that I could not trust the need to look at a script, and that I wanted to fully identify with the crowd.

I folded into this speech my 'patented' presentation of the *two streams* (I choke up thinking about it, as I type this paragraph) and drew my remarks to conclusion with:

In our battle for spiritual freedom and political liberty, let it never be said that any one of us did not hear, or that we did not see, or that we did not speak. We must gallantly defend those principles that are America.

Change must come if the greatness of America is to be restored. We must rearm America so that we can live in peace. We must rebuild America if we are to be prepared for the 21st Century. And we must control government if we are to improve the quality of life.

Change must come.

How will it come, how can we bring the change that is needed? As I pondered that question, from the depths of my soul I felt these words - "Let Reagan be Reagan ... Let Reagan be Reagan."

As I started the second time to say, "Let Reagan be Reagan," Constitution Hall erupted (or rather exploded) with cheering, yelling, clapping, and a thunderous response. That expression resonated at the core with these political appointees and they adopted it as their brand.

I share this story (and the full text of this speech in the Appendix) because it reflects the political values your mother and I tried to live out in those Reagan years. There were days of exhilaration and days of challenge.

I want to share one other speech (with full text in the Appendix) because it too reflects our values and created a reaction we all continue to live with. It is the speech I call "... In a Town Nearby."

The Assemblies of God meets every two years at General Council, a gathering of thousands of their pastors and wives. They had wanted me to speak to them at their August 1981 Council meeting. But I declined their invitation because I would not let any of our appointees (including myself) leave Washington until we had brought about a significant portion of the change the President had promised.

This was disappointing for them because they had made me their 'poster boy' in that I was the first of their denomination to serve in such a high ranking office. I phrase it that way specifically because when the *Washington Post* ran a profile on Reagan's Cabinet members, I was listed as a member of the Assemblies of God. I got an early morning phone call from a Republican United States Senator. After identifying himself on the phone, he told what the paper had claimed about me and wanted to know if it was true. When I confirmed that I was a member, he seemed astounded and said, "And you admit it? I frequently attend their churches, but I would never admit that I was a member." We are a marked family, maybe a peculiar family.

I accepted their invitation for the 1983 General Council meeting, believing that by this far-off date I would have brought about most of the changes we wanted for the Reagan

Revolution. I started framing in my mind what I wanted to say, 'preparing spontaneous answers.' It became something I was looking forward to, so I started writing things down almost a year before I was to address the General Council. When your mother saw me writing down notes, she knew I was taking this speech seriously. I seldom wrote out what I was going to say. When your mother saw the zero draft of my intended remarks (that is the draft before the first draft that you should let anyone see) she said flatly, "If you give that speech, you will lose your job." I kept working on it and she helped me with it - a whole bunch.

In those years the 'holiness' group of evangelicals thought they should live a totally separated life and not be involved in politics. Politics was frequently thought to be 'dirty.' I thought we should be involved and wanted to give this speech, recognizing of course that my intended remarks went far beyond any responsibilities I had in the Reagan administration. I structured the speech showing what happened when the European Christian community, living *in a town nearby,* failed to get properly involved in political life during the years leading up to Hitler's reign of terror.

The speech was dramatically received by the thousands attending the General Council and had a big play in the national press.

After that speech, TV camera crews started following me all around Washington, filming every minute of any public appearance. At that time I was a 'headline getter' and thus Congressmen wanted me to help raise political funds for them; organizations wanted me to appear before their groups. If we felt these speaking engagements were part of our mission for the President, I would do them. Sometimes several speeches a day.

After several weeks, Doug Baldwin, head of our Department of the Interior public relations (and my friend since 1962 when we joined forces on the Milward Simpson campaign) spoke to a CBS crew that was always following me around. Doug said, "Why are you following the boss to all these Washington events? He gives basically the same speech every time." They responded, "We are under orders from New York. They believe anyone who speaks as frequently as your boss does, will say something he shouldn't, and we are instructed 'to get his blood splattering on the wall.'"

And they did (politically speaking).

In an appearance before a natural resource group of the United States Chamber of Commerce, I made a politically incorrect statement and 'executed' myself from government service. I had been under pressure to appoint a commission to investigate a coal leasing program of the Department. I appointed an extremely competent group of people and it so happened that it was also a very diverse group. This was to my benefit, because we were always under pressure to bring greater diversity into the government. To reflect that diversity when introducing the new commission I announced, "I have a black, a woman, two Jews and a cripple." The national press went wild and the liberals came after me with a vengeance, because I had used the word 'cripple' instead of handicapped. (The politically correct term today, I believe, is physically challenged.)

The five newly appointed commissioners tried to defend me, but Senator Bob Dole, the Republican Majority Leader, was determined to drive me out. In a face to face meeting, I looked him in the eye and said, "Bob, you were wounded in World War II and it crippled your arm and hand, but it has not handicapped you as a man or as a United States Senator." Still the unrelenting attack and hostile press, on top of the previous months of battle, consumed all my inner strength and I asked to be relieved of my command. The President refused to accept my first two attempts to resign, but at my third effort he realized I had no more inner strength.

Therefore it was a surprise to me that speaking invitations kept coming in.

I signed with a New York speakers bureau that secured speaking assignments with business organizations and universities. It was an easy way to make good money and I enjoyed meeting the variety of people. I wrote a book, *The Courage of a Conservative* (published by Simon & Schuster), which gave me lots of resource material for speeches.

I particularly liked going to college campuses. The students were always excited and eager to learn and the professors, almost always, were left wing crusaders. The mixture was ripe for an explosion. And if it did not happen on its own, I would sometimes set it up. Frequently during the question and answer session (which I liked the most) a left wing professor, wanting to put me down or ridicule me, would say something like, "Based on some of your comments, it sounds as if you believe the Bible and do not accept the science of evolution." At this point I would make the 'pregnant pause' even longer and then say, "That's right. I do not believe in evolution. I am not a racial bigot."

At that moment I had the total attention of everyone in the room and everything was frozen. On a college campus you can say almost anything except charge that someone is a racial bigot. Then looking straight at the professor, I would say, "Professor, by your question, I assume you believe in evolution. You then have to make a determination as you look at your students: which one has evolved more? Are the Asian students superior or inferior to the Black students; the Latino students superior or inferior to the white students. I know your text books show man evolving out of the goo to an upright, hairy, dark animal, then to a long armed black animal, and eventually to a blond Aryan. That is bigotry of the worst order. As a Christian who believes the Bible, I believe that God loves us all, '… red and yellow, black and white, all are precious in His sight … '."

Many times the professor, with his liberal devotees, would slink out of the room cursing mad, while the Christians and conservatives gathered around, thrilled that someone had been able to stand down the liberal professor.

Use the opportunities you are given to deliver your message, expecting a response.

I was sorry to see this era of my professional life phase out. But interest in a speaker's opinions wains in proportion to the time that person is out of public life.

GOD TURNED AWAY FROM ME

I t is not always easy to know when God is talking to us. And sometimes we are confused as to whether it is God, the devil, or our own imagination.

Many times I have heard what I thought was God and would then test the spirits as we are told to do in 1 John 4:1, 2.

> *Dear friends, do not believe every spirit, but test the spirits to see whether they are from God, because many false prophets have gone out into the world. This is how you can recognize the Spirit of God: Every spirit that acknowledges that Jesus Christ has come in the flesh is from God.*

Frequently it costs you something to obey God. And almost always there is a terrible price to pay when you disobey God.

My battles have always been about control. I liked being in control and thought I was good at it. God asks us to surrender and yield to Him. It has been a constant battle since the day I chose to follow Jesus. (I explain in the chapter "The Pride of Life" that it was years later God spoke to my heart on this matter of control, while I sat in a canoe on the Snake River).

I grew up in a politically active home and developed great ambitions for elected office. I did everything I thought appropriate to position myself for a political life. Right out of law school, I was campaigning for the man who was elected to the United States Senate and who took me to Washington as his General Counsel and Legislative Assistant.

During that campaign the Lord spoke to me with great clarity and purpose. *I was never to seek elective office.* It made sense to me then because during the years I served Senator Simpson, Doug and I made an image of the man that was bigger than life. Senator Simpson often remarked, after a trip to Wyoming, that he was received better as a senator than he had been treated as governor.

In the late 1960s and during the 1970s, I held several key government positions in the executive branch of our government by appointment of President Nixon's Secretaries of the Interior and by President Ford. I learned how Washington worked and I worked Washington very successfully. In 1980 I was asked to join the Reagan Cabinet. We had huge successes bringing massive change to the way the Department of the Interior had been run. After I 'executed myself' from government, we returned to Wyoming.

Soon a United States Senate seat opened up. There was a legitimate need. I believed that no one was better prepared to serve Wyoming than I. With the experience, the know-how, and the ability to raise the money, I could get elected. I started to lay the ground work to run for election to the Senate. Things started to fall into place for me. I was thrilled: I had seen the need and I was able to fill it. I was needed. But I had failed, neglected, or ignored the responsibility to ask God's permission or direction. I had not remembered God speaking to me thirty plus years earlier not to run for elective office; not to create a political image for myself.

Soon a politically-motivated investigation was aimed at me. My dream of being a United States Senator vanished. I was consumed by the battle at hand.

I hired Washington lawyers. We responded to every inquiry. When the Democrat/Clinton lawyers could not find any wrong doing, they told my lawyers they would drop the investigation if I would agree to plead guilty to one felony. Because I did not believe I had committed a felony crime, I was unwilling to agree to their demands. In response they said in effect, "If Watt will not plead guilty to some felony, we will ruin his reputation and destroy him financially." Over professional advice to agree to their terms, I stubbornly refused to agree to lie by confessing to something I had not done.

I thought it would be easier to explain to you grandchildren that I was in jail because the jury would not believe me, than it would be to tell you that sometimes you just have to lie to get out of a tough situation. Each of you has been wrongfully punished at some time because a parent or other adult did not believe you, so you would have understanding.

The lawyers continued to pursue their politically-motived efforts to destroy me. After several years and a mounting legal debt of over $1 million, a new prosecuting counsel was appointed. I demanded that he review my case. After doing so he agreed to drop all the felony charges, if I would plead guilty to a misdemeanor.

I balked at that until the lawyers handed me a book, three inches thick, titled *Federal Misdemeanors*. I started thumbing through it. I saw I was guilty of many federal misdemeanors. To drive from our home to the post office or to the airport, we traveled through portions of the Grand Teton National Park and I usually drove faster than the posted speed limit. I cut teepee poles on Shadow Mountain without a federal permit. I dug up little evergreen trees growing on Forest Service land to plant in Larry Ashenhurst's front yard in Wheatland, never having a permit from the federal government. These are all federal misdemeanors.

We found an obscure violation that all could agree would be face-saving to the Independent Counsel's office. I had personally answered by mail a request for information from the grand jury that was now deemed *influence, a federal misdemeanor.* If a lawyer on my behalf had sent the letter, it would have been permissible.

During these years of battling the politically-motivated prosecutors, I cried out to the Lord for protection. The prayers of David as presented in the Psalms became real to me.

I turned to Psalms 30 in the New Living Translation, verses *6-12*:

When I was prosperous, I said, 'Nothing can stop me now!' Your favor, O LORD, made me as secure as a mountain.

Then you turned away from me, and I was shattered.

I cried out to you, O LORD. I begged the Lord for mercy, saying, 'What will you gain if I die, if I sink into the grave? Can my dust praise you? Can it tell of your faithfulness? Hear me, LORD, and have mercy on me. Help me, O LORD.'

You have turned my mourning into joyful dancing. You have taken away my clothes of mourning and clothed me with joy, that I might sing praises to you and not be silent. O LORD, my God, I will give you thanks forever!

I realized the Lord had turned His face from me because I had disobeyed what He told me thirty years earlier. *I was not to seek an elective office* and I had prepared to do so. I was in disobedience. And He turned away.

I had hit rock bottom. I pled for His mercy and His forgiveness.

And He, the Almighty God, looked again upon me with His favor - with mercy - and with blessings. I was grateful and thanked Him.

Be alert. Do not do as I did, trying to control all dimensions of my life, but seek His guidance and be obedient to what the Lord instructs you to do.

Selah!

PREPLANNED
SPONTANEOUS ANSWERS

Sometimes it is necessary to have pre-planned answers or comments because you know that you are going to be asked *the* question.

Sometimes it is necessary to have pre-planned answers or comments because you know you will not know the real answer or do not want to answer the question.

Sometimes you are asked a question and you know that person really does not want to know and will not listen, even if you answered their "How are you?"

Sometimes you feel you ought to comment but do not want to.

And other times you should not say what you know to be the truth but should use discretion.

I have collected an array of answers that have helped me get through the tough moments. Here are a few examples:

When I was in high school, I asked my dad what I was to say when some woman was showing off her new baby. I told my dad they all looked the same to me, but that I felt I was supposed to say something nice. He told me the art was to look at the baby and then look in the mother's eyes and say with real feeling in your voice: **"Now there's a baby that's a *real* baby."**

"It is a true statement. The mother is thrilled. Everyone smiles and you are off the hook," my dad said.

******

Your mother and I, in partnership with several couples in Jackson, created and founded the Arts for the Parks program. It was a successful national competition for artists to paint a picture of a landscape or wildlife in a specific National Park. The first prize was $100,000 and thus it drew many entries, at fifty dollars an entry. Your mother helped organize the fifteen hundred or so pieces of art. (I set the size limitation at 24 inches by 18 inches because that was a good size for the FedEx delivery.) Needless to say, the competition attracted all types and all qualities of art.

The selection process was not at all difficult in the first round. Like all selection processes (where there are lots of entries) you simply have three piles: yes, maybe, and no. I was particularly good, as was everyone else, at identifying what went into the no pile. But Patti, one of the artists who was in our partnership, called me aside and said, "Jim, your judgment is good, but your vocabulary is not acceptable."

She then gave me the following instruction: Unlike the real world, in the art world beauty is in the eye of the beholder. Everyone's judgment is deemed good and acceptable; there are just different preferences. We know this is not necessarily true, but it is the standard for the art world. In looking at a piece of art that is just terrible, you are not to say so. You are to say something that will not offend the artist.

I was to cross my arms, cock my head, squint my eyes and say, "Very interesting." Or, "An unusual use of color." Or some other nonsense. That way I would not have to lie, but neither would I offend anyone.

Apparently inoffensive comments are important in the art world as well as in other arenas of life where I have not done very well.

******

I am frequently asked, "What do you do?" I have struggled to find a meaningful answer.

One of the best is, "I don't know, but it takes all day." This empty answer gets a good laugh and allows me to move on, because it means absolutely nothing.

The most meaningful answer and one that opens many avenues for conversation is, **"I am pursuing the toughest task of my life: trying to become a human being, as God intended, rather that a human doing."**

A human **being** is dependent upon relationships, not titles, activities, or events.

******

I have embarrassed myself several times when seeing a woman I know from church at the doctor's office or hospital and saying some trite thing like: "How are you?" or "What are you doing here?" I really do not want to know; I am just trying to be friendly.

With the same intent, women have greeted me in the hospital waiting room or at the doctor's office, as I sit there waiting for the nurse to call me because of a prostate problem or urinary tract infection. What am I to say?

Or what am I to say when someone, with good intentions, is politely asking me about your mother's limitations because of hypokalemic periodic paralysis?

I asked our friend Connie, who sits at the receptionist's desk at our local hospital, what

I should say in such instances. She has had more experience than anyone I know in this field. Connie said the best and most satisfying answer she had heard was simply, **"So-so."**

It really works!

"How are you feeling?" With a little rocking hand motion, "Oh, so-so."

"Why are you here?" "I've been feeling just so-so."

"How's your wife?" "So-so."

It says absolutely nothing. No further questions are asked. It is totally satisfying to 99% of the people and helps you move on to other subjects.

******

My first job out of law school was working in the campaign for Governor Milward Simpson who was seeking the United States Senate seat for the state of Wyoming. I learned 'to work the crowd' by watching him. His objective was to have as much personal contact as possible with each person in the room. He told me to follow him and to keep him from getting involved in any long conversations with any one person. When he was talking, I was to interrupt and say something forcing him to move on to the next person.

When I first did this, he flared at me and turned to the person with whom he was talking and said something like, "I am sorry he is making me move on." The person glared at me for being so rude. So I did not interrupt the next conversation the Governor was having. He then said to the person, "Excuse me, I have to tell Jim something." He pulled me out of the room and lectured me that I was to move him quickly through the room and not pay any attention to his protestations. Thus, I was perceived by the people to be rude **but was pleasing to the Governor for whom I was working.**

He was a colorful and charming man. He was a father figure to me. When he was asked how he was doing, he would frequently say, "I feel more like I do now than when I first got here." Most people were so worried about making a good impression with the Governor/Senator that few understood or cared what his answer was. Those who did pay attention gave it a hearty laugh.

The Senator was the best at preparing spontaneous answers. In facing a difficult situation he would say, "I need the prevision of retrospect."

When we would receive a lot of mail asking the Senator to vote a particular way on some innocuous bill, I would take two stacks of mail (vote yes and vote no) into his office, brief him on the bill, and ask him what he wanted me to tell the people. He would give my briefing at least a half a second's consideration and say, "Tell them I'll do the needful." So I would write the letter saying, "Dear xx, Thank you for your counsel on____ . You can be sure that I will do the needful." Everyone was happy. They believed the Senator agreed with them and he had the freedom to do what he wanted.

I in turn adopted this useful wisdom. On my desk in jobs following the one serving the senator (and to this day), facing anyone who comes to the office, is a little sign giving the same instruction:

DO THE NEEDFUL

Senator Milward L. Simpson moving my admission to the United States Supreme Court - 1967

******

Preplanned spontaneous answers is a concept that is very important. When I was in public office, I gained a reputation for being 'fast on my feet.' What they did not know was that I was prepared - prepared in advance of the occasion. I had read that Winston Churchill spent half his time preparing spontaneous answers. **I spent lots of time thinking about what to say in anticipation of a variety of circumstances in which I imagined finding myself.**

A MAN WHO KNOWS
HIS POSITION

While serving in the Reagan Cabinet, I attended a White House luncheon with a large number of America's religious leaders. There were Roman Catholic priests, Bishops and Cardinals; Greek Orthodox priests; Rabbis; Methodist and Presbyterian ministers and leaders; plus all the other known leaders of religion in the nation. Of course, the easily recognized ones were there: Billy Graham, Jerry Falwell, Pat Robertson, Bill Bright, and the head of the Southern Baptist Convention.

Those of us 'in the know' always smiled at how easy it was to get attention and a crowd at the White House. All you had to do was have the White House telephone operator call and say to the recipient, "The President would like you to _____." With that one sentence the captains of industry, the leaders of the labor unions, and the governors of the states would drop what they were doing, change their schedules, and come to Washington or wherever the president asked. They all said something to the effect, "When the President calls you have a duty to _____."

As I sat in that luncheon, I looked over the crowd and thought even religious leaders are driven by the desire to be known and to be seen in places of power. Power seems to be an alluring force that few can resist. It has been my achilles heel. I was also thrilled to be there.

I 'worked the crowd' before and after the luncheon. I liked meeting the religious leaders of the nation. I already knew many of the political leaders. As I took inventory of who I had seen and with whom I had visited, I realized that the one big name I had not seen was Oral Roberts.

When I returned to my office, I placed a call to our friend and the president of the university where our kids were attending. When Oral came to the phone, I explained that I had just come from the luncheon with all the religious leaders and had missed him. I told him that I could secure for him an invitation to the next such event and that I would like to see him included in such activities. (In my opinion, if there ever was a person deserving recognition as a religious leader, it was Oral Roberts.)

Oral responded, "Jim, I received the invitation. God has not called me to that type of ministry." And he changed the subject. He started talking about something else.

I was stunned. Here was a man who did not seek the acclaim of the powerful or the mighty. He did not need to be seen or acknowledged by political or other religious leaders. He was content to be used of God in whatever capacity God called him. He knew his position in Christ. He was a humble man and thus powerful.

I admire and honor Oral Roberts.

Some years later (2010), I was telling this story to a long-time friend, author, and former evangelist, Mike Evans. After nodding his head in affirmation and admiration, he told me the following story on himself.

Mike had attended the very luncheon at the White House that Oral did not attend. He knew it was going to be a full house with many of the nation's religious leaders and all the key Reagan people in attendance.

In an effort to get a favored seat, he came to the White House early and stood in line to be one of the first in the door. He knew he wanted to sit on the aisle where President Reagan would be coming in. He was fortunate to be able to find just the right table and the right chair to be seen by all those in attendance, and by the President as he came in and went out. He knew he would be noticed. (Mike stands at about six foot six inches. And with his shock of black hair, is noticed wherever he goes.)

When the luncheon was over, everyone stood as usual as the President left the room. When President Reagan walked past Mike's table, he paused and reached to take Mike by the arm as he said, "Will you walk with me as I leave the room?"

Mike's dream had been realized. The President noticed him, recognized him, singled him out of the large crowd, and even asked Mike to walk with him. Mike was glowing. Everyone in the room would be watching and would see Mike as he walked out of the room with the President of the United States.

For reasons Mike did not know, President Reagan was heading out to the helicopter to go somewhere and kept Mike with him. As they walked past the entire White House press corps with all the cameras clicking, Mike was thrilled beyond words.

The President stopped, took Mike's right hand in both of his and looking up into Mike's face said, "George, I cannot tell you how much this has meant to me."

The President abruptly turned, walked to the helicopter, and as he went up the stairs, turned and waved to "George."

George!? Mike was crushed! As he stood there in total dejection, he realized all of his motives were wrong. When he got to his office in Ft. Worth the next day, he called the White

House staff and asked that his name be taken off the invitation list.

Oral knew his position. God privately exposed Mike's nature and flawed hope that public notice equaled favor with God. Instead, God taught Mike humility and that **the most powerful positions are the ones God places us in, not the political positions we seek out.**

Mike is a good friend and a humble man, so humble that he can tell this story.

GOD IS OUR SOURCE

While we were living at the Paintbrush home on the golf course in Jackson Hole and Eric and Becky were missionaries in Singapore, Oral and Evelyn Roberts came for an evening dinner with us. My sister Judith and Evelyn were seated on one side of our long table, while Oral and your mother and I were on the other.

Oral knew Eric and his ministry. He considered Eric one of 'his boys' who was trusting God and who was taking seriously the mandate God gave Oral, "... to go where My light is seen dim, where My voice is heard small, and My healing power is not known - even to the uttermost bounds of the earth. Their work will exceed yours, and in that I am well pleased."

I remember vividly Oral telling us that he had preached all his life that God is our Source. He said, "I have preached and believed it with every fiber of my being and I want you to tell Eric that I have lived it 20% of the time."

My respect and admiration for Oral soared. He was a humble man. He could **state a truth without embarrassment or demanding attention or pretending to be perfect.**

Selah.

Our Wyoming Senator Cliff Hansen and family at my FPC swearing in ceremony - 1975

WILLING TO DISSENT

Three or four months after being sworn in as President Ford's appointee to the Federal Power Commission (a quasi-judicial commission which regulated the interstate sale of natural gas and electricity), I was explaining the job to my dad. He had been a successful, small town, Wyoming lawyer. After telling him about the tremendous shortages of natural gas and the increasing costs to the consumer, I shared my strong beliefs that we needed to bring about change. And that unfortunately, my views were not always being adopted. Thus, I explained, I would have to be dissenting more and more to the opinions of the Commission.

After a slight hesitation Dad said, "That's a good idea! Most of what you government men have been doing has been wrong all along. You just as well be dissenting to it."

Since then I have felt free to continue speaking out with an independent voice.

Dad spoke to a principle that became an important part of my life style. In so many categories of life, I am in the minority. My social and political values are not shared by the majority. My Christian commitment and life style definitely reflect a minority position. And so it is with you kids. We are a peculiar family. The scriptures tell us we are to be witnesses. **Do not let your minority status limit your life. We have a duty to speak out about what we believe to be the truth, whether it is a dissenting point of view or not.**

DO YOU KNOW JESUS?

In February of 1964 I was a content man: thrilled with my job, working in Washington for the United States Senator from Wyoming, and married to a wonderful woman. We had two adorable children (Erin three and a half and Eric two years old). We lived a good life – a religious life, a productive life. We were satisfied in every way.

Your mother was prompted to pursue spiritual things. She attended a meeting at a big Methodist Church and came home with a brochure telling of the Full Gospel Business Men's Fellowship International (FGBMFI) convention coming to town. *She determined I should go and check it out.*

February is a difficult month for a Senate aide, but your mother was determined that I should go and learn about this FGBMFI. I was not against doing so, but on the other hand it did not have a high priority. She called mid-morning to remind me to go straight from work to the major hotel in Washington to check out the convention. She called at noon. She called late in the afternoon and again about the time I usually started for the door. By then I realized it would be easier to go to the hotel and check things out than it would be to go home.

When I got to the downtown Washington hotel at 16th and K Street, I found the lobby crowded with men *and* women wearing name tags at the top of a long white ribbon filled with the initials FGBMFI – but I thought I was going to a business MEN'S meeting? I asked for directions to the meeting room and was directed to the grand ballroom. I looked into the room and found it crowded and hot. Men were passing me carrying chairs to meet the needs of the people packed into the ballroom - over fifteen hundred people.

I started walking down to the front of the room and was stopped by a big Black man (in those days we used the word Negro) and he said, "Brother, there are no seats down front. We're bringing chairs in as fast as we can." I looked at him with amazement. Why did he call me 'brother'? Couldn't he see that we were not related? I smiled and said to him, "Oh, there will be a place for me," and pressed on.

Sure enough on the third row there was one empty chair. It was mine. I sat down and was completely fascinated by the businessmen who would come to the 'mic' and speak for five minutes about their lives and how they had been impacted by a man named Jesus. I had never heard 'personal testimonies.'

Seated next to me was a short man with a great big nose. It seemed that every time an important point was made, he would speak out in a loud, deep voice, "Praise the Lord" or "Hallelujah." I thought it was very disruptive and rude. But he just smiled when I scowled at him.

The testimonies were very captivating. Men telling how they lost a business or job; a wife and children left them; alcohol was consuming their lives; and then they met a man named Jesus. And because of Jesus their marriages were restored, their children loved and respected them and their businesses prospered. I was impressed. But there was a formula. Success – failure – meet Jesus – and success. I liked the success part but had no identity with the other parts of the formula. I wondered how a person could ever get so messed up. My life was certainly not like theirs.

I was watching with interest as the convention leader moved to change the order of the meeting. I had a great seat immediately in front of the speaker's podium so I could see the facial expressions and body language. He called for a song to be sung. The piano player started on one side of the wide stage and the organist on the other. But just as the crowd began to sing, Demos Shakarian (the man I would later learn was the International President of the organization) moved to the microphone and said, "Wait. There is someone here who wants to know Jesus." Everything stopped.

When he said those words, my heart was gripped. "Do I know Jesus?"

My mind raced with that question, "Do I know Jesus?" As my mind was racing, I heard him say something to the effect of, "I want all Christians to close your eyes and bow your heads and be praying. Now will those who would like to know Jesus just slip up your hands."

With that last sentence, the battle in my mind widened and the questions and answers went back and forth. "Do you know Jesus?" "I had years of perfect Sunday school attendance." "But do you know Jesus?" "I was president of my high school youth group in the United Church of Christ." "But do you know Jesus?" "They elected me president of the state-wide church youth group." "But do you know Jesus?" "We were active in the college Presbyterian group at the University of Wyoming." "But do you know Jesus?" "I was chairman of the Methodist social concerns committee while in law school." "But do you know Jesus?" "We are now attending a Baptist church." "But do you know Jesus?"

I realized that I did not know Jesus.

But how could I admit I did not know the one who started my religion? "I am a Republican," my mind battled. I decided that maybe I should raise my hand as the man had suggested. Then I remembered that I had found a seat in the third row right in front of the podium and if I were to raise my hand everyone of the fifteen hundred plus in the grand ballroom would see me admitting that I did not know this man they called Jesus. Fortunately, I also remembered the leader had asked all Christians to close their eyes and bow their heads. I was relieved. No one would see me raise my hand; and if they did, they would not dare admit it. I carefully slipped my hand up, letting the leader know that I wanted to know Jesus.

With my hand in the air, I heard the man say, "Now all those who have slipped a hand in the air, please stand up." I witnessed my first miracle – I was standing. Standing up in front of all those people and now it did not matter. It was no longer important what they might think.

But when he continued, "I want all those who are standing to come to the front of the room," my mind was filled with the battle again. The same battle I struggled with just moments before, "Do you know Jesus?" Again all the answers kept sweeping through my mind telling of my outstanding religious record.

Always those religious answers were followed with the question, "Do you know Jesus?"

I decided to go forward.

That first step was the most difficult step of my life. I was all alone. I had to step out – all by myself - with no one helping or encouraging me. It was a step of determination. The second step was easy. The Living Christ was there to escort me to the front of the room with one hundred and nineteen others. One hundred and twenty persons stepped forward out of a crowd of more than fifteen hundred people.

I repeated the words of prayer as I was instructed, only later to learn that those words were what these people called the 'sinners prayer.' I had never heard such a prayer.

That night after driving home to suburban Maryland, your mother knew the moment I walked through the door of our apartment that a difference had come over me. It did not change my lifestyle or my vocabulary. I was just different on the inside. I struggled for many months to understand why there had been a change.

I had gone forward that night because I had wanted to know Jesus. I was not aware of any sin in my life. I had not done anything I considered bad, and yet there was a signifi-cant difference in my being. I kept wondering why. Someone suggested that I should read the Bible, but I did not see what relevance it had to the 1960s – the Space Age.

Out of curiosity, and more than seven months after going forward in the Sheraton Carlton Hotel ballroom, I decided to read the Bible. No one told me what to read, so as a good lawyer, I started reading at the beginning, with Genesis. As I continued into the sixth chapter, I read "that the Lord was grieved that He had made man." When reading that phrase, I had a magnificent *revelation* from God.

I immediately understood about the First Adam and his act of sinning that brought sin to all his descendants and thus humanity's 'sin nature,' which required the Second Adam (Jesus) to be sacrificed for the remission of all sin for all those who call upon His name. It was an immediate understanding. It was caught, not taught. It was revealed, not learned. I understood the plan of salvation and realized that I, too, had been and was a sinner.

I had become a believer – a follower of Jesus; not just an intellectual Christian, or a cultural Christian, but I had committed to a new life in Christ. Now I could answer that question: "Yes, I know Jesus."

THE PRIDE OF LIFE

Joe and I were going to canoe at the Oxbow on the Snake River. I wanted to hear what he had to say. Joe was one of the members of the three Bible study groups in Jackson I started in the summer of 2002. Three groups: one for those of us older than sixty, The Old Wine in Old Wineskins; one for those about forty years of age, and one for those in their twenties. We were studying the life of Joseph who set many wonderful examples and faced some real hardships.

On Thursday morning, we old men – Don Brunk, Doug Eggers, Mike Dailey, David Wilson, and Jim Watt - would discuss the principles set forth in the life of Joseph and one of us would invariably say, "That reminds me of the time ... And God met me and delivered me out of the situation." It was a time of rich sharing and focusing on the mighty power of God to involve Himself in the specifics of our lives. I was always encouraged, blessed, or challenged

Getting ready for the Oxbow

as I heard the life stories of my close friends.

At lunch time on Thursday, the men in their forties gathered to discuss the same lesson on Joseph. As they – David NeVille, Todd Seeton, Scott Christensen and Brad Richardson - would see the biblical principle set forth, one or more would lean forward and ask, "Jim, how do you deal with that situation? That is just what I am now dealing with in … " And we would all join in the discussion on how to live out the principle and make our lives pleasing to God. It was a very rewarding time to see good men eagerly pressing in, applying the biblical principles to their lives.

Later in the afternoon, I would meet with the younger men. As they recognized a principle, one or another would pipe up and declare, "No problem," quote a scripture, and be on to the next issue of the book.

The following year I did not activate the younger group. There is no need presenting biblical principles to those who know it all. In fact, I know of a good Christian man who does not bother to share his powerful Christian testimony with other businessmen unless they are going through bankruptcy or divorce. He says it is a waste of time. As long as a man can do it by himself, he sees no need for God.

However, on one of those Thursdays with the younger guys, we were discussing sin – lust of the eye, lust of the flesh, and the pride of life. Joe Palmer had done a study on the matter. I found him to be very interesting. Afterwards I asked Joe if he could teach me more about the 'pride of life.' He responded that he would be glad to do so. I suggested that we go canoeing early in the next week so he could outline the subject for me.

After we drove forty minutes to the Oxbow on the Snake River in the Grand Teton National Park, we unloaded the canoe and pushed off. I said, "OK, Joe, tell me all about the 'pride of life'."

He responded, "Well, it's about wanting to control all the circumstances of your life."

"Tell me more," I quickly replied.

"That's about all there is to it."

With disappointment and a little disgust, I said, "You mean we drove all the way out here to go canoeing so that you could say **that the sin called the 'pride of life' is about wanting to control one's life**?"

I had wanted to discuss the subject. Study it.

But in the quietness of the Oxbow, watching the big, white pelicans paddling around, the osprey fishing from above, and a big, black bull moose browsing among the willows, God spoke to my heart.

There was no need for discussion or study of the sin called the 'pride of life.' I was an expert of sixty plus years – an accomplished sinner. I knew all that one needs to know about the 'pride of life' – trusting oneself instead of trusting God.

I felt the warm tears roll down my face. In the quietness of the moment, I whispered, "Forgive me."

God heard me.

Selah!

SURRENDERING TO ORTHODOXY

In the Spring of 1964, your mother started attending a six A.M. Saturday morning meeting in a Presbyterian Church. It was a growing group led by Bob Topping, the Presbyterian minister. It attracted people from Washington, DC, Northern Virginia, and the Baltimore and southern Maryland areas. They were learning about a phenomenon called the baptism in the Holy Spirit as evidenced by the speaking in tongues. She came home excited. I stood my distance. But soon after your mother received the experience of the baptism in the Holy Spirit, we did start attending a Sunday evening pentecostal service at the Church of God at 3456 Pennsylvania Avenue South East, in the District of Columbia.

That pentecostal church was a loud church. I kept my hands in my pockets and was very alert - with my eyes wide open all the time, even during the prayer time. We were only visitors. After the service got started, the Pastor would say, "Will the choir please form." Almost the entire congregation, including your mother, would move up into the choir loft leaving me, you two little kids, and two or three old ladies sitting in that big sanctuary looking at the 'congregation' now in the choir loft. They sang with gusto. It seemed that they usually sang "I'll Fly Away" and I wasn't sure but what they would do just that.

In the fall of 1964, Senator Simpson sent me to Wyoming to help in the Barry Goldwater presidential campaign. After traveling with the Republican candidates through Sheridan, Cody, and Jackson, I called and reported to the Senator that Goldwater would not be elected and could not carry even Wyoming. The next day his personal secretary called me and advised me not to call in again for some period of time because the Senator was furious that I would think that Goldwater would not carry Wyoming and the national election. She feared for my job. But that was not my biggest concern.

My real concern was a spiritual one. Your mother had been reading some private letters sent exclusively to some friends written by two women from Massachusetts or Michigan, who were teaching that Jesus was going to return at *noon* sometime in October of 1964. And further, that He was going to take with Him only those who had received the gift of speaking in tongues.

She was concerned for me and you kids because we had not yet been blessed with speaking in tongues. I was more concerned than she was because, while I did not believe any of this stuff, I wasn't totally sure it was wrong. Each day in October I was anxious about the midday period because I did not know whether Jesus was coming at noon Eastern Standard Time or noon Rocky Mountain Standard Time. When November first came up on the calendar, I was the most relieved guy in America! Your mother was also glad to have this 'goofy' false doctrine exposed.

After the 1964 election (Goldwater did lose, even Wyoming), I returned to Washington and the family. I picked up a book, *They Speak with Other Tongues* by John Sherrill, an Episcopalian and the then editor of *Guidepost Magazine*. He told of his experiences that led to receiving the baptism in the Holy Spirit. I identified with his life.

The next Sunday I decided to skip the Baptist Church service and go to the morning service of the pentecostal church. Your mother stayed home with you kids; you had colds.

In that Church of God, when the preacher called the congregation to prayer, everyone stood and started praying aloud, simultaneously. And they were loud. Very loud. Almost all the attendees raised their arms and prayed in the Spirit. It seemed very confusing to me, but the people were 'lost' in prayer and did not seem to listen to each other. In fact, it was so loud that you could not even distinguish the words of the person praying next to you.

I decided that I would try an experiment. I had never taken my hands out of my pockets nor shut my eyes in the several times we had visited this church. So I decided to see if anyone would notice (or if it would cause embarrass-ment to me) to raise my hand. I first slowly moved my hand from my pocket to the lapel of my suit jacket. I carefully looked around. No one seemed to notice. I then reached up and scratched my ear and again it drew no atten-tion. With a new boldness, I raised my hand straight up. Nothing happened. I then took the other hand out my pocket and slowly, but cautiously, raised it.

As I looked up at my outstretched arms, I realized I was making the universal sign of surrender. You would have thought that any cowboy from Wyoming would have known that. With that surrender I had a new desire to go to the altar and ask for the baptism of the Holy Spirit. I had to wait for the sermon to be over and for the preacher to call those who wanted to come forward to do so.

As soon as I could get to the altar at the front of the church, I was on my knees with my arms reaching toward the heavens. I felt a presence that I had never experienced before and then I heard myself speaking in a language that I had never learned. With tears streaming down my face, I felt a thrill never before experienced as I prayed in this new language. After a few minutes I was emboldened and wondered what would happen if I opened my eyes. Nothing. I continued praying in the unknown language. I tried lowering one arm - then both arms; and then raising them. I decided to stop praying and then to try to start again. Could I? To my thrill I realized I was in charge of the expression and that the Holy Spirit would never do anything to embarrass me.

That was the beginning of a new walk with Christ. In February 1964 I had been baptized into the Body of Christ by the Holy Spirit (born of the Spirit). In November of 1964 I was baptized into the Holy Spirit by the Lord Jesus Christ. It took a while for me to come to the realization that when I had raised my hands, surrendering to the presence of the Holy Spirit, I was experiencing the identical thing the first generation of believers experienced. It was orthodox Christianity.

WORTH DOING POORLY!

During one of the visits with the grandchildren in Broken Arrow, I found the back leg of the lounge chair out by the pool was broken, still broken. It had been in the same condition the year before. It was a fine lounge, and an expensive one at that. But how to fix a molded aluminum, fancy chair leg is not easily determined. Particularly by a talented analytical like my favorite son-in-law, Terry, who does many things and does them well.

Realizing that the lounge had been broken for 'some time,' I went to the garage, got a hammer and a broken broom handle. I drove the broom handle up into the leg of the chair and sawed off the handle at the right length. The ugly blue handle sticking out of the aluminum fluted leg did not look pretty, but it made the lounge useful.

Laura came bounding out and asked, "What are you doing, PaJames?"

I told her I was fixing the lounge chair. She said, "It sure is ugly."

I said, "Sit in it." Laura jumped in the chair and said, "This is great." And I responded, "It sure is ugly."

With a big smile and gleaming eyes she said, "Looks don't matter; it works." Laura understood a principle of life.

As each of the grandchildren (seven counting Jackie) came out to see what was going on, I showed them how the broken chair, except for its looks, was as good as new. And I paraphrased the principle of life as set forth by G.K. Chesterton, the English theologian and entertainer:

If something is worth doing, it is worth doing poorly.

My father taught me the opposite: If something is worth doing, it is worth doing well. The trouble with that principle is that most of the things in our home never got fixed. If you have to do something 'well', and you do not know how or you do not have the proper tools, things just do not get done. The fear of failure paralyzes your mind and your desire to take any action.

The business management books and the consultants tell us that 'good is the enemy of the best.' It sells a lot of books, but the truth is if we think we have to be the best at everything we undertake, then little is initiated. I note with interest that the senior management team of Facebook pushes the concept aggressively. Their walls feature posters declaring "Done is better than perfect."

Remember Chesterton: **If something is worth doing, it is worth doing poorly.** 'Good enough' is sometimes good enough.

ROMANCE - CUT FLOWERS AND GOING OUT TO EAT

I n 1982 I traveled extensively on Department of the Interior business. Because of the controversy that swirled around me, I became a big draw for Republican fundraisers. The Republican National Committee asked if they could add to my official schedule some events and dinners benefiting the Republican Party and some of the individual candidates who were seeking office that year.

I was glad to help in any way possible to advance the Reagan Revolution. So I told them I would do as they asked if they would pay for your mother's travel expenses (the government did not pay for accompanying spouses and we could not afford to pay the cost of travel for her). It was reported that I was second to the President in raising funds for the Party in 1982.

She treated each formal event that year as another celebration of our twenty-fifth wedding

50th Wedding Anniversary

anniversary, even though the actual date was in November. She was wonderful at making the simple beautiful and the official personal without anyone else knowing it but the two of us.

In the preceding twenty-five years, and as a matter of fact for these following twenty-five years, I was not and am not good at romancing my wife. Your mother has tried to coach me and I have read books, but the only thing that I have learned is that women like cut flowers (not potted plants) and that they like going out to eat. I have really tried. I really do try.

During this year-long, much celebrated twenty-fifth wedding anniversary, we were guests of honor at a very formal restaurant in California. As we sat at a big, round table filled with eight high-ranking California Republicans, our close and dear friend, a rotund and bearded man, stood. Out of the large vase in the center of the table he plucked a beautiful cut flower and graciously handed it to your mother.

I thought she was going to swoon on the spot. I had never seen her so completely swept off her feet. She simply was overcome with this thoughtful but simple expression of admiration, shown by our friend.

A few days later, still in California, we found ourselves seated in another expensive res-taurant with a group of politicians. I quickly noted there was, just like several days before, a large vase of cut flowers in the middle of the table. Wanting to act before someone else would 'sweep your mother off her feet,' I stood up, plucked a flower from the vase, and presented it to your mother with a big smile and a glow of satisfaction. I, too, could demonstrate an act of romance for the woman I love.

With a look of consternation she said, "Sit down and put the flower back." For some reason I just don't know how to pull off this romance thing.

Some years later while living in Jackson Hole, we had made it a custom to celebrate your mother's August birthday at Jenny Lake Lodge, a very special place. That year I made the reservation, which is required, and set up our 'date' for her birthday luncheon. I bought a beautiful potted plant and hid it in the trunk of our car and drove my 'bride' the thirty plus miles to the Lodge. After being escorted and seated at our white linen-covered table, I excused myself. Your mother thought I was going to the restroom, but I was retrieving the beautiful flowers. I returned to the dining room with confidence and pride to give your mother this beautiful gift. I set the potted plant down in front of her; she pushed it aside and kept talking. Not a thank you. Not an "Oh, how beautiful." I tried not to show my pain of rejection.

After the meal was finished as we started walking out of the dining room, I spun around saying, "Let's don't forget your flowers!"

She said, "Oh, just put them back where you got them. We're not going to take their flowers."

Now we laugh at ourselves. Back then, I could not get it right, no matter how noble my intentions.

Cut flowers and eating out are romantic if done at the right place and the right time. Maybe it's the when and how.

DETERMINED
TO FINISH STRONG

I n March of 2004 Erin and her two daughters, Kara and Laura, came to Arizona for Spring break from college and homeschooling. It was a special time.

One morning while we were still in our pajamas, I was sharing some of the family heritage and traditions I wanted them to capture. I picked up from my office desk a framed bulletin we received when visiting a Lutheran church. It features an old man's arthritic hand gripping a cane and a quote from my 'life's verse', Hebrews 12:1.

Therefore, since we are surrounded by such a great cloud of witnesses, let us throw off everything that hinders and the sin that so easy entangles, and let us run with perseverance, [endurance, discipline, determination, and

*dedication] the race [that God, himself]
has marked out for [each one of] us.
[Watt's amplified version].*

I told the girls that I was determined to
finish 'the race' strong. I went on to explain
that since my father died in 1990, I have visualized him in that "great cloud of witnesses",
looking down on me; cheering when I made a
right decision and hurting for me when I did
something stupid.

All of a sudden I was choked up. Hot tears
were streaming down my face and I was
embarrassed that I could not finish the story.
I looked up through tear-blurred vision and
saw my three girls crying with me, their dad
and granddad, about the greatness of God.

Again I went to my desk and got the only
plaque I display in our home. It was given
to me at the end of the summer men's Bible
study group, just before your mother and I
headed south for warmer weather. I read it to
the girls:

Jim,
Thank you for running the race with us.
By His grace we will finish Strong!
Dave, Don, Doug, Mike,
Summer 2002

I explained that I had walked with these four men for all my Jackson Hole years as we struggled and rejoiced in our individual and collective walk with Jesus Christ. I called that special group of cherished friends, The Old Wine in Old Wineskins.

After the final summer meeting that year, as we embraced and said good-bye, Dave lingered. When he was sure we were the only two standing in the parking lot, he started sharing with me. Dave had been a faithful friend for many years; he and his wife came to stand with your mother and me at one of my darkest hours. He truly had a pastor's heart. He had been a pastor and president of a Bible school. He was a great soul winner and I had seen God use him many times. I loved him.

Dave asked if I felt that maybe one of us would not be here when I returned the next summer. I was surprised to have him ask that question because indeed those same thoughts had been rolling through my head during our Bible study that morning. We discussed the matter for a while and even agreed upon who the Lord might 'call Home' during the winter months.

In the summer of 2003, we returned to our Jackson Hole home and when The Old Wine in Old Wineskins Bible study group gathered on the regular Thursday, only four of the five chairs were filled. It was my friend Dave who was not there.

He had not been 'called Home' by the Lord.

I went on to explain to Erin, Kara, and Laura that Dave had simply tired of his 'race' against the pressures of the world: sickness, finances, dishonest Christians, backbiting Christians, family problems. I did not know all that the devil used to beat down my friend Dave. I tried to phone him on many occasions; I emailed him. He did not respond. I drove out to his home and simply waited for him. When he came, we embraced. We visited for a long time. He was convinced that what he was doing was right. He never returned to the fellowship. He has found new friends and divorced his wife of some forty years.

With a choked up voice and more tears, **I told my girls that I am determined to run the 'race' God that has set before me and to finish *strong*!** And with the grace of God will do so.

We promised each other that morning that we would each finish our individual 'race' and BE THERE in heaven, waiting for the others.

There is a nice postscript to this chapter. My friend Dave now lives in Arizona, not far from where I lead another men's Bible study. He is an active member and a loved brother.

DIVERSITY, AMBIGUITY AND PARADOXES

In about 1972 when I was heading up the Department of the Interior's Bureau of Outdoor Recreation, I attended a cocktail party and was visiting with a Democrat Congressman, John Dingell. John and I had an unusually good relationship over the years, even when he was about to file Contempt of Congress charges against me as the Secretary of the Interior for defending President Reagan's presidential powers. He is still in Congress as I write this piece and has been for 58 years. He said, "Maturity is the ability to accept diversity and ambiguity." I have found it to be true.

I would add to that sentence one word. "Maturity is the ability to accept diversity, ambiguity, and paradoxes."

The world is full of paradoxes, particularly the Bible. A paradox is two statements that are true but totally inconsistent with one another. Our God is a God of peace. Our God is a God of war. Our God is a God of love. Our God is a God of justice.

God is capable of dealing with diversities, ambiguities, and paradoxes, so step back and accept them for what they are and do not try to resolve all the conflicts of the world.

And further, on a totally disconnected subject, **never take advice from a man who does not limp.**

I have found there are always those who want to give advice and tell you what to do or how to handle a particular situation. Unless they have encountered something similar to your situation, they lack the understanding to give meaningful advice.

As your mother says, Jacob wrestled God for control and lost by a tendon! From then on he limped, but he walked with God. I look for people who have had an encounter similar to my situation and seek their advice. They probably limp, but they have survived.

Ready for the ride - Leilani, Eric and Erin

IT'S WORTH SEEING, BUT IT'S NOT WORTH GOING TO SEE

Your mother and I were determined to give you children as many experiences as possible. When you were grade school age, one of our excursions was into Pennsylvania Amish country to learn more about the ways those people lived. On a drive one day, I stopped (uninvited) at an Amish farm house and walked right up to the kitchen door where I could smell the baking bread. Wiping her hands on her apron, the woman of the house came to the door. I explained that even though we had come from rural America, our kids were now living in the city and had never experienced gathering eggs. "Would it be all right if the kids went into the chicken house, reached in under the hens and gathered the eggs for you?" She was delighted with our interest and took you kids by the hand. Away you went. You were not as delighted as she was. But it was an experience.

I frequently embarrassed you two kids (and your mother) as I would insist on just one more experience. When I stopped an Amish man driving a spirited horse pulling his black buggy, to ask if he would take you kids for a ride, you recovered from your embarrassment very quickly. You saw the envy of other tourists as we all smiled down from the buggy and the horse was heard clippity-clopping along.

On another occasion we took a vacation driving south into the state of Virginia. (This was a homeschooling project before we had ever heard the phrase: making every observation a learning experience.) We stopped at every factory and industrial plant we could find. I would go in and explain that I had with me my six and eight year old children and wanted to show them how people made a living in America. Most the time we were rejected. But some of the managers invited us in to see what was going on. And some of the plants even had planned guided tours for visitors like the four of us.

We saw how shoes were made, cigarettes were manufactured, clothes were sewn and sized. We watched them cut and hang tobacco. One manager was so pleased that we wanted to see his manufacturing facilities that he took us on a long – long - tour of turbos and converters, used to make thread. From that moment on you kids were afraid that I would make you go to another plant with turbos and converters – whatever that meant. To this day, you *still* remind me that you do not want to see any more turbos and converters.

One afternoon was very humid and hot. We were dragging, but I learned there was a peanut butter manufacturing plant just forty miles down the road. I stood at a street corner with you two, Erin on one side and Eric on the other, each asking to go to a motel so you could get out of the heat and just rest. A local man gave us directions to the peanut butter manufacturing plant.

After getting the directions I asked, "Is it worth seeing?"

The man could see how tired and drained all of us were, particularly you kids. He shook his head and said, "It's worth seeing, but it's not worth *going* to see."

Immediately we found a motel for the night. (But I have since wondered how they *do* make peanut butter.)

"It's worth seeing, but it's not worth *going* to see." Those words have been a guiding principle in my life as it relates to many, many things. They are words to be remembered.

First day of school at Capitol Christian Academy 1968: Erin, third grade and Eric, first grade

HOW TO PICK A CHURCH

After committing my life to Christ in 1964 at a Full Gospel Business Men's Convention, I became a regular at the Washington, DC, Regional convention. It was an important part of my life. Each year I would visit with an older man from the western part of Virginia, Brother Simpson. In those days we addressed one another as 'Brother' or 'Sister.' Seldom did we use first names. Brother Simpson belonged to an old country church. He told me (maybe the better words are that *he directed me)*, "Brother Watt, never go to a church that does not use the name of Jesus and preach the power of the blood of Christ."

We have some Wyoming friends who moved to Wickenburg for a host of family reasons. They were burned out and looking for a different church environment; one they could fit in and enjoy. After visiting most of the Protestant churches, their bright, little five or six year old granddaughter Lexie said, "I want to go to a *real* church."

They returned to our church where they could get orthodox Christian teaching like it was taught in the first generation church.

It is important to remember ol' Brother Simpson's admonition: **"Brother Watt, never go to a church that does not use the name of Jesus and preach the power of the blood of Christ."**

Selah.

ASSUME THE PERSON
AGREES WITH YOU

After I became a follower of Christ and had been sharing my testimony about receiving the baptism in the Holy Spirit, a Canadian man counseled me: "In talking to others about praying in tongues, or Jesus, or being baptized in water, or anything else, always assume the person with whom you are talking shares your conviction and belief. Never assume that they might not agree with your position."

This is great wisdom. **Always assume the person with whom you are talking shares your conviction and belief. Speak from a positive and inclusive position, whether your subject of conversation is religion, politics, or business**. If you do this, you will not sound defensive or in doubt. If there is a disagreement between the two of you, the other person is put on defense. It is always easier to be on offense than defense.

Success

is satisfying the one to
whom you report.
With your actions of
today, can you hear
the Lord saying,
"Well done.
I am pleased with you."

SUCCESS AND SIGNIFICANCE

As a young man I was always a hard worker, always hoping for a better job. In some instances I tried to get my boss promoted so that I could have his job. I found that my boss always liked that idea. Fortunately or unfortunately, it never happened. But my quest was always for more power and more authority.

I had no entrepreneurial skills and was never focused on making money. However, sometimes I feared that I would not have enough money.

There is never enough power for a man who craves power, nor is there enough money for the one who is driven "to make only a dime more." There is always someone who has more power or more money. And yet we are driven to compare and compete.

When meeting with my men's groups in Jackson and Wickenburg, we were frequently dealing with 'the drive for more.' That is how men define 'success' and 'significance.' We struggle to find it in the business world, the academic halls, the sports world, sexual conquest, or the political arena, and other odd places.

Once a man determines that he is successful in his world, he wants to be thought of as significant (admired) by his peers. In the world, there is always a need to compare and compete.

Peace of mind on these matters of success and significance only comes when we find ourselves in proper relationship with Jesus Christ. That is success. Significance is realized when we understand that the Creator of the universe, The Almighty God, has chosen to live His life through us and our unique circumstances.

In my struggle to bring understanding to these issues, I created (with a little help) a certificate that puts it in proper perspective and presents two questions.

As I wrote and re-wrote the lines of the certificate, I was reminded of when I was in high school working on a federal dam site at Glendo, Wyoming. Our foreman, who wore a red hard hat, was called Smokey. We wore white hard hats. We reported to Smokey. When we saw Smokey coming, we all stepped a little faster and worked a little harder. Success was satisfying Smokey.

Success is satisfying the one to whom you report and most of us report to more than one authority. Thus, the first question that must be resolved is whether or not we are reporting to the right authority or authorities.

The second question: **With your activities of today, can you hear the Lord saying, "Well done. I am pleased with you."**

After framing the certificate and seeing it by my bedside, my prayer life and behavior changed. Knowing that success and significance is determined by a right relationship with Christ, I go to bed each night expecting the Lord to speak to me about what I have done that day, hoping I have pleased Him.

JAMES WATT'S GOD

In the early 1970s a wonderful and close fraternity brother flew to Washington, DC, to see us. He had been divorced and was living with a girlfriend. When the girlfriend learned Don was coming out to see us, she advised him that when he returned they were going to get married or he was to move out. He did not know what to do. We had known Don and his first wife very well. We counseled and witnessed to Don until late into that evening. I drove him to his hotel room and said good night, knowing that he would catch a flight out early the next morning.

A couple days later he called to thank us and to tell us what had happened.

After going to his hotel room, he sat on the edge of his bed and bowed his head and prayed: "I am praying to James Watt's God. He said if I asked You, You would make it clear to me by morning whether I am to marry X or to move out. Amen."

When he got up the next morning he knew with certainty that he was to move out. And he did.

We stayed in frequent contact with Don during the following years, witnessing to the faithfulness of God and sharing our lives with him. Fourteen years later he called while on a business trip in Minneapolis. Your mother answered the phone and recognized his distinct voice as Don simply said, "I have accepted Him."

The One True God has many names, too many to number. He can be identified as Almighty God, Maker of Heaven and Earth, The Lord God my Provider, The Mighty Warrior, The Prince of Peace. He is also known as James Watt's God, Don's God, Leilani Watt's God, Erin's God, Eric's God, Terry's God, Becky's God, Joel's God, Kara's God, Ethan's God, Laura's God, Elliot's God, Trent's God, Ian's God, and Kiersti's God. The list goes on and on.

Selah!

NO MORE BLACK CHICKENS

In 1997 we attended a Youth With a Mission (YWAM) five month Crossroads school in Kona, Hawaii, and Ukraine. Your mother and I returned to Kona the following three years, for schools and just to be in Hawaii during the winter months.

We took a Spiritual Warfare class (a bummer) and a Humanities class that was fantastic. The next two years your mother took Introduction to Biblical Counseling and Foundations in Art. I spent time with friends and got involved with Mission Builders who help establish YMAW bases. In 1998 I went on a Mission Builders' trip with Troy Stremler to Thailand and Nepal.

As I was walking through a Brahmin village, a talented young Nepali named Mohan shared his Christian testimony. His grandmother had learned there was healing power in the name of Jesus. As word spread of the miraculous healings experienced as a result of her prayers using the name of Jesus, leaders of many villages in that mountainous region asked Mohan's grandmother to come and pray. Mohan traveled with her and saw the many miracles - people being healed as she called upon the name of Jesus.

But the grandmother and Mohan continued to go to the temples to offer blood sacrifices for the forgiveness of sin and to appease the many gods that influenced their lives. They could not afford goats or sheep so they took black chickens to the temple as their sacrifice. Black chickens were thought to be more effective (and thus were more expensive) than ordinary red or white chickens. Mohan's grandmother was always poor because any time she had a little extra money it was used to try to appease the gods by offering up black chickens.

Several years after Mohan and his grandmother learned of the healing power of Jesus, another group of YWAM'ers visited the area. These young people told Mohan's grandmother that this Jesus she knew as the Healer was Himself the only Son of the Most High God who did not need to be appeased. Instead as a gift to all people, God accepted the blood of His own Son as the perfect sacrifice that would take away sin. Mohan's grandmother would need no other sacrifice. Ever. No more black chickens. No more poverty.

Mohan and his grandmother accepted Jesus as Lord and Savior. Now Mohan spends his life in Nepal telling of Jesus the Savior, Jesus the Healer, Jesus the Lord of all.

I was stunned to hear Mohan's story. To think that in this modern age people still believed that they should sacrifice animals for the forgiveness of their sins and to appease their gods. I was ignorant of the blood sacrifices and rituals of other religions. Had they never heard of God's gift or had they rejected God? Blood sacrifice was the right idea, but its meaning had been corrupted. It was beyond my comprehension.

The idea haunted me for months. I needed to see for myself.

In 1999 your mother, David NeVille and I, joined Troy on a missionary trip to Nepal and India. When we arrived in Kathmandu, Nepal, I renewed my friendship with Mohan. I asked Mohan if he could take us to a temple where we could see the priests sacrificing (slaughtering) the animals. The religion of Nepal is officially Hindu but Mohan told us the Buddhist, Animists, Pantheist, and Muslim influences were all stirred into their belief system.

At first Mohan showed embarrassment and hesitancy about taking us to such a temple. Animals were sacrificed at the temple only on Tuesdays and Saturdays - Saturday being the big day, he explained. And further, it would be a forty-five minute ride and he could only take your mother on his motorcycle. I suggested that we could go on Tuesday and hire a taxi and the four of us could go – Mohan, your mother, David and I. He thought that would be too expensive for us. But I persisted and told him to make the arrangements.

The taxi ride up the mountain was most interesting. As we passed through the many little villages, the people stared at the three white faces in the taxi. The farmers laid their wheat stalks on the paved roads and as our tires rolled over them the grain was thrashed out and later swept up for their use. Women sat along the roadside with hammers breaking rocks into gravel to sell for making the roads. We learned the Nepali rock crusher is women with hammers.

After about thirty minutes into the drive, we noticed a growing number of people moving along the road, headed in the same direction: walking, on bikes, in carts pulled by oxen, and in a few cars - nice cars. At the temple site there were large parking lots and then stalls and stalls with venders selling doves, red chickens, black chickens, goats, and sheep. Lots and lots of chickens, mostly red.

As we started walking down the stone paths that led to the temple, we moved with brown skinned people of all economic positions in life. One of the couples that drew our attention was very stylishly dressed and looked as if they could have been walking down a street in Hollywood, California, instead of a mountainous village in Nepal. They probably were in their mid-forties. Their car, a new blue Mercedes-Benz, was driven by a man who appeared to be their chauffeur. The well-dressed man held the leash and headed down the stairs to the temple with the goat peacefully following, not knowing what was to happen to him (the goat)!

The four of us walked past the long lines of people (hundreds) waiting with their animals for their turn to pay the priest to slit the animal's throat. We watched the blood spurt out on the altar as the animal's heart kept pumping for those brief remaining moments. There were at least four and probably six priests slitting throats of the goats and chickens as fast as they could bleed out the animals. The blood flowed down from the altars and into the rock paved channels, like a small mountain stream in Wyoming.

Here in this modern age how could there be the slaughter and spraying of blood on an altar? It looked like a scene out of the days of Elijah. A jet flew over some thirty-six thousand feet up in the air. The thought went through my mind: *Those people in the plane have no idea what is going on down here.* How could

**Coming to sacrifice to their gods.
Nepal - 1999**

anyone? I could not comprehend what I was seeing.

Mohan said the crowds were bigger on Saturdays!

After the people had paid the priests, they hired a worker to take the dead animal and dress it out so they could take the meat home to eat.

The blood was running off the altars, and off the shoes and clothes of the priests; it was on the walkways where we were; it covered the workers; it filled the paved channels; and it was for naught.

As we started walking up the stairs out of the temple area, we could see into the faces of the hundreds of people waiting their turn to sacrifice their animals to their gods. Neither your mother nor I could comprehend such a scene in this modern age. As I looked into what seemed like an endless line of brown faces with lifeless dark eyes, I said to no one in particular or maybe to God: **"All they want is to have their sins forgiven."**

Selah!

MARRIAGE COUNSELING

In the spring of 2004, I felt the need to fly to Portland to visit with a Youth With A Mission friend I had been mentoring on a long-distance basis over the last few years. Eric Stasak was a successful stock trader and we frequently talked about buying and selling shares of stock. I set up the meeting for the purpose of learning how he did it so successfully, but down deep inside I knew there was a greater reason.

Eric and his wife Dalene and their two children were a delight. Eric and I spent hours and hours on our new computers, buying and selling, using Interactive Brokers.

It is an exhausting way to make a living – physically sitting at the computer at ALERT for hours (Eric said the distance between scratching my nose and having my hand on the mouse amounted to hundreds, if not thousands of dollars, and he was right.) It was intellectually exhausting because one must make dozens of decisions in a matter of seconds;

and it was emotionally draining because one must continually fight conflicting forces of the fear of loss or the greed for more. I loved it. (But I did quit after about six months. It was more than I could handle.)

Dalene prepared a picnic supper for us and we went out to the beautiful banks of the Columbia River. As we were playing with the kids and enjoying the great day, Dalene shared that she sometimes felt threatened by Eric's comments. She feared that if she did not behave just as he wanted, he would not love her or even might desert her.

I heard myself saying, "Dalene, Eric can't leave you or desert you. He has promised God and your parents and all the friends at the wedding to love you and that it was 'for better or worse, through sickness and health.' Every time he introduces you to people as his wife he is recommitting those vows of marriage. How recently has he introduced you as his wife?" She responded something to the effect of "just the other day and he always tells people that I am his wife."

I smiled and said, "You have no fear of being rejected because **every time he has introduced you as his wife, he has renewed the vows of marriage**. And with each introduction that many more people are aware of his promise to love and honor you." She looked at Eric as if to say, "Is that right?" I quickly turned to Eric and said, "Isn't that right, Eric?"

With eyes as big as silver dollars, he said, "That is right. That is what I have meant."

Later in the evening, he got me alone and thanked me for the counsel. And over the months he has thanked me again and again. Each time I laugh and remind him that while I think it is perfectly correct counsel, the words spoken by me never came from me. I had never heard them or thought of them before the three of us heard them along the banks of the Columbia River.

Selah!

RIYADH

In 1971 I was a Deputy Assistant Secretary of the Department of the Interior and had line responsibility over the Office of Desalinization. However it was the Department of State that named me as the contracting officer of a contract they had made with the Saudi Arabian government to build with Saudi money, a desalting/electrical generating facility in Jeddah, Saudi Arabia. The Office of Water Desalinization had been given the responsibility to oversee the design and construction of building the facility, using contractors from the world market place.

An American company, *Burns and Roe*, won the design and engineering contract. The Germans got the boiler contract; the Japanese the generator contract; the Dutch the construction contract; and the Pakistanis the labor contract.

It was to be a seventeen month contract. I was named the contracting officer during the forty-fourth month of that contract. Obviously there were problems: The closing of the Suez Canal due to the 1967 Six Day War between Israel and Egypt, plus other issues.

After several trips to Holland concerning the complicated contract, I finally went to Jeddah for final resolution of the problems. I soon was well acquainted with the Saudi King's son (one of many), the Prince who had the lead responsibility for the Saudi government with regard to the desalinization plant. I negotiated with the Prince and after finally getting his approval and signature on the final settlement with the Dutch, I was instructed to be at the airport at 8 A.M. the next morning. We were going to Riyadh, the capital of the country, for final approval.

I thought I had been dealing with the final authority but learned that the Prince reported to a higher government official, not of the royal family. It was my new assignment to get the signature of the Prince's boss before final settlement would be made.

I was thrilled to be going to Riyadh. My assistant, a desalting engineer who had been counseling me on all the technical matters, and I got on the plane which was filled with men. About half were wearing the robes of the Saudi nation. I noticed as we flew, men in western clothing would go to the restroom and come out dressed in the apparel of the Saudi nation. By the time we landed, my assistant and I were the only ones wearing pants – at least the only ones wearing pants that could be seen.

Immediately upon arrival in Riyadh, we were taken to a government office building and served 'tea.' There behind armed guards (robed men standing at attention with their rifles in hand) we were offered small cups of a sugary thick, syrup-like drink, while we waited for the real decision maker. I was expected to make the presentation to him. He was a very bright guy and a graduate of University of Southern California. What had taken me hours and hours to explain to the Prince was grasped by this guy within minutes and the 'deal' was done.

It was a thrill to be escorted around Riyadh. It was as if we had been transported back in time to the days of Abraham and Ishmael – but with cars. As we drove down paved streets of the city, we were delayed as Ishmael's descendants, dressed just as I believe he would have dressed, herded flocks of sheep with their big fat tails dragging behind them. It was explained that the tails stored the energy that allowed the sheep to get through hard times.

Upon successfully concluding this nightmare of a problem with the Saudi Arabian government and returning to Washington, I had to explain the agreement to the State Department officials. My success in Saudi

Arabia apparently had regional consequences, because now I was being asked to travel to Israel as a guest of that country.

It seems that when the American Israeli lobby learned that the United States government was going to take the latest and best desalting technology to Saudi Arabia, they demanded like treatment for Israel - of course, with one major difference. They wanted the U.S. taxpayers to pay for the similar desalting plant in Israel. After their aggressive lobbying, the Congress appropriated the necessary millions of dollars. President Nixon did not want to spend that money and had it sequestered by Office of Management and Budget and the State Department.

The experience gained in Riyadh and at the Department of State taught me that titles (royal or governmental) can be impressive, but in business and in government, **the power rests with the person who has the authority to control the money.**

THE WAILING WALL
OF JERUSALEM

Although the Department of State sent me on another assignment, God had the last word. Golda Meir's Israeli government was convinced that if the United States government would send a representative to their country and get an understanding of their water problems, the United States would *want* to build the desalting plant in Israel. I was selected to go with the advanced understanding that when I returned, I was to write a report saying it was *not* in the best interests of the United States to build such a desalting plant – that it would not advance our understanding of desalting technology. (At that time we called it a desalinization facility.)

So in 1971 with an engineer from our Office of Water Desalinization, I went to Israel. We were guided around Israel for ten days learning how the Israelis deal with the water issues concerning the Golan Heights, the Jordan

River, the Dead Sea, the Red Sea, and the Mediterranean Sea, plus their irrigation and municipal water needs. It was a fascinating trip. Our guide was instructed to show us the water resource base and water problems of the nation. He wasn't instructed to give us a sightseeing tour. But I wanted that, too. And he was gracious to schedule in some of the great places of Israel. It was truly a magnificent trip.

The one site I anticipated seeing more than anything else was the western wall of the Temple - the Wailing Wall. It had just been opened up to the Jewish and the free world with the 1967 Six Day War.

I knew in my heart that something of major significance would happen if I could or would be allowed to go near that great Wall and touch it. I had seen the pictures of the Jewish wearing their prayer shawls and 'bobbing' back and forth as they prayed for the first time in almost 2000 years before the Temple Wall. It was a powerful spiritual symbol for the world to see how this newly acquired freedom had impacted the devout among Jewry.

I knew it would be important for me, too. My mind was not limited in imagining all the great things that God might do if I were privileged to touch that Wall as I prayed in the Spirit (in tongues).

On the day our guide allowed us the free time to go to the Wall, I moved with trepidation. We were asked to wear a skull cap (the yarmulke) as do the Jewish, if we were to approach the Wall. I put on the black, construction paper cap that had been stapled together for tourists like me. The men went to one side of the fenced wall and the women to the other.

I approached cautiously and slowly. Because of my high expectations, I was observing everything I could. The stones were huge and between the cracks were rolled up prayer requests stuffed in by the hundreds. As I approached the Wall I was praying in the Spirit. I reached out my hand and lightly touched the Wall with the back of my fingers.

It was stone cold.

The voice of the Lord spoke to my heart, **"These stones are not holy, for the holiness of God dwells in the hearts of the believers."**

Selah.

BE LED NOT PUSHED

I n the summer of 2004 God made meaningful to me His teachings on shepherding
the flock. I grew up in Wyoming, the fifth
largest sheep producing state in the Union. We
have big bands of sheep (1,000s) and within
each band there are several herds (100s). A
sheepherder is charged with moving the herd
and keeping it safe from coyotes and other
predators, like eagles. He moves the herd from
the rear. When he sees some sheep straying
off or going in the wrong direction, the sheepherder rides his horse out and chases them
back into the herd; or sends his dog out to
yap and snap at the sheep to run them back
to where they are supposed to be.

Too often this describes my walk with the
Lord. I try to stay in the 'green pastures,' but
frequently I see something that attracts me
and I go astray. I start off on my own and the
Shepherd has to come and get me, or send
out other saints, or angels, to push me back
to the flock, and to the green pastures. If I do

not respond to the good forces, the hounds of hell will chase me until I recognize them and return to the flock or am destroyed.

In the eastern part of the United States and in the Middle-East, they do not herd their sheep. The shepherd *leads* the sheep in small groups. He knows each sheep and they know him and his voice. They will only follow the voice they recognize.

The scriptures tell us that we are to follow in the steps of the Good Shepherd. We are not to go it alone. **We are to follow in His steps and listen for His voice.** And when we do, we will have peace and security. The hounds of hell will not prevail.

THE SMARTEST KID
IN THE DUMB CLASS

Upon graduation from high school in 1956, it was assumed that I would go to the University of Wyoming and eventually to its law school. I had been saving my money for college since I was just a little kid. It never occurred to me or the family that there was another college I might consider.

I was given a scholarship for tuition by the County Commissioners. (Your mother got her scholarship because she was a scholar – the smartest one in our graduating class of fifty-two students or at least fifty-two kids.)

The university had a fraternity and sorority program that most students considered essential if you were to be important on campus. In addition, I had decided for my future political ambitions, I needed to belong to a fraternity.

During the first week of school, Rush Week, each of the Greek societies would have parties to impress the incoming freshmen. You got to pick which of the fraternity parties you wanted to attend. Each of the fraternities would also assign one of their members to 'check up' on you and help you through the first week of school. Of course, he would try to win your friendship for his fraternity.

Then on Saturday morning each freshman could go to the big central building, the Student Union, to see if he/she had received an invitation to join a fraternity or sorority. It was a big deal. Of course some of the students would get many invitations and some would get none - not even one. (Your mother never attended any Rush parties. She had no interest in sororities.)

Back at the dorm all the boys would be sharing thoughts and ideas and asking, "Which fraternity are you going to join?"

I was being 'rushed' by several of the fraternities. Each night I would get with new and old friends to learn what they were going to do. I knew many of the smarter and sharper boys because many of them had gone to Boy's State after our junior year in high school. (They had elected me Governor of Boy's State and I was selected to go to Boy's Nation in Washington, DC). I was watching with a keen eye to see where the 'smart guys' were headed.

It soon became apparent that the best and brightest were going to pledge with the Sigma Nu fraternity. They wanted me to join them.

I was more than confused. I did not know what would be the right decision. And of course at that time I thought it would be the most important decision of my life. I decided late Friday night that I would not pledge any fraternity but wait for a week or two, as the rules allowed, and make a decision after I could see where the 'good guys' were.

With hindsight, that was the right decision. **When confused or in doubt – don't.**

During the next few days it became apparent that most of the good friends from Boy's State had pledged Sigma Nu, just as we had anticipated. I then realized I did not want to compete with them for positions in the fraternity, or for grades, or for political positions on campus.

I decided to join the Alpha Tau Omega fraternity. They had a pledge class made up of a bunch of good guys - but no scholars, no outstanding leaders, and no one who had attended Boy's State. I decided it would be better to be 'the smartest kid in the dumb class' than to be just one of the guys competing in the smart class.

The result was that as the university was organized, each of the class honorary societies was composed of two members from each of the fraternities and sororities, plus some Independent students. Your mother was always the outstanding Independent in each of the honoraries. She was really smart. I was just 'the smartest kid in the dumb class.'

Selecting the two best scholars for honorary societies from the Sigma Nu house created lots of friction because there were some really talented boys there. Some were taking very hard courses and some were taking easy courses, but the highest grade averages determined who represented the fraternity in the university-wide honorary societies.

But at the ATO house it was always very easy to pick the two students to be named to the honorary societies. It was James Watt and one more who might qualify. The result was that I was selected to be a member of Sophomore (Omicron Delta Kappa), Junior (Iron Skull), and Senior (Phi Epsilon Phi) honorary societies and was elected president of each of them.

I did not have the best grades at the university, but maybe I was the 'smartest kid in the dumb class.'

YOU ARE NOT ALONE

In May 1994 I was sitting in my office at our Paintbrush home when I received a phone call from a good friend from the Reagan years. After a delightful exchange of pleasantries he said, "My lawyer wants to talk to your lawyer."

I laughed and said, "I have no lawyer." My friend responded, "Jim, you are going to be indicted next week for criminal activities concerning your Housing and Urban Development (HUD) business. You had better get a criminal lawyer."

I did not take him seriously and responded with a comment like, "I wouldn't want a criminal lawyer. I would want an 'innocent lawyer'." He kept talking to me and convinced me I should call a lawyer and find out what was going on.

That started the deepest, darkest period of my life.

During the Clinton years, the Independent Counsels were creating so much misery for the Democrats that, to balance things out, they

The thought is always with me

went on a 'witch hunt' for Republicans. I was one of their targets. When they could find no wrong doing in HUD business activities, they investigated ten years of our personal and corporate tax returns. And interestingly, the IRS came to our defense.

A few years before, we had been subjected to a congressionally instigated IRS audit. Your mother had done such a good job with her redundant records that the IRS praised our multiple years of filing and did not ask us to amend or change anything for those many years.

When the 'out of control' Independent Counsel lawyers came after us, I will always believe the IRS defended us because they were determined that nothing would be found by those Independent Counsel lawyers that they had not already audited and approved. IRS had done their work thoroughly and correctly. There were no errors or mistakes to be found.

Failing to find any wrong doing with our HUD business interests or tax returns, the Independent Counsel turned to congressional testimony and alleged perjury - felonies. It was a miscarriage of justice from the very beginning, motivated by politically corrupt Democrats.

During those dark and lonely months, many of our 'friends' took a walk, but our real friends and family rallied to my side. The Psalms and prayers of King David were food for my soul.

Eric was on assignment with missionary duties in Singapore, a whole fifteen hours ahead of Jackson Hole time. Frequently, I received an early morning email from him with statements like, "Today was a good day, Dad. You're going to get through yours just fine." Those messages always brought comfort to my inner being. Erin sent me a small yellow card she hand-lettered in bold black that read, "You are NOT alone." No words have been of more comfort. To this day, I carry it in my billfold. The support of your mother, you kids, family, and friends carried me so that I could put my trust in God.

After twenty months and the expenditure of millions of tax payers dollars by the government lawyers, a new Independent Counsel was appointed. Over the full opposition of my lawyers (and just days before we were to go to a jury trial in the District of Columbia), I insisted on a face to face encounter with the new man. At that meeting, to everyone's surprise, all felony charges against me were dropped.

I was not alone.

Selah !

PRESENTING MY WORLDVIEW

How we live our lives is determined by our worldview. The degree of commitment to one's worldview can vary greatly, however.

The concept of a worldview was new to me when it was introduced in a school at Youth With A Mission. And I was surprised to learn that everyone has a worldview whether they know it or not. Your mother and I grew up in an agricultural community where there were strong Christian principles; where individuals were expected to show initiative, responsibility, and accountability; and where there was a broad respect for the life and property of others. Almost everyone shared those same basic values. It was the worldview of our community.

In recent years, a significant segment of our nation's population has taken on views contrary to Judeo-Christian principles. Views that reflect an attitude of entitlement linked together with open disregard for individual responsibility, a disrespect for private property, and a devaluation of human life. These changes have been coming over a period of time since World War II with the New Deal, the Great Society, and the sexual revolution of the 1960s.

Thus today, in a meaningful conversation where opinions differ, it is useful to understand the core values, the worldview, of participants. The most significant factor in a person's worldview is the presence or the lack of a religious belief system. Those with different religious belief systems will have clearly differing worldviews.

I have used the following outline in the college classroom, in Sunday school, at Rotary Clubs, and during informal gatherings:

There are 7 billion people in the world. (I am a "rounder." In presenting a worldview I always round numbers and tell the audience that I am generalizing, but that I will be right 90% of the time.) And we are presented with this question:

If you were on an island in Hawaii and a huge volcano erupted spewing lava that covered the airfields, filled in the sea ports, and eliminated communications, who could you count on to rescue you?

Would the 1.3 billion Chinese (Buddhists, Taoists, Ancestor worshipers, Atheists, and Communist influenced) come to your aid?

(Now you get the class to start guessing and you will no doubt need to coach them.)

The ANSWER: No, the Chinese never go to help anyone. The word China means 'Middle Kingdom' and the Chinese believe they are at the center of the world. They believe every one comes to them. This is their worldview.

Would the over 1 billion Hindus come to your aid? (Ask the class.)

The ANSWER: No, they would not want to get in the way of the 300,000 plus gods of the Hindus. And if they did, they would be challenging karma which would require you to go through the same thing in the next incarnation. This is their worldview.

Would the over 1 billion Muslims come to your aid?

The ANSWER: No, if Allah wills it, why would you work against Allah? They do not want to go against Allah. And everything that happens is Allah's will – good, bad or neutral. This is their worldview.

Would 1 billion Tribal, Pantheists, and New Agers come to your rescue?

The ANSWER: No, the gods would not allow them to do so. If the gods of the volcanoes wanted to erupt, why challenge them. This is their worldview.

Would some of the more than 2 billion Christians come to your aid?

The ANSWER: Yes, I am my brother's keeper. This is the Judeo-Christian and Western civilization worldview.

Once you have discussed this subject of worldview with a person and get a 'feel' for their religious values, you can usually predict how they will line up on the political issues of the day.

The issues such as abortion, gay marriage, entitlements and some welfare programs are frequently labeled political battles. But in fact they are conflicts over which worldview will prevail. The constant battling over those values can cause a subtle encroachment on deeply held values and cause compromise if we are not alert to what we hold of primary importance. Who and what is at the center of our worldview: God? The Bible? The individual? The federal government?

Our commitment to biblical values will place us in the minority position. We who make that commitment are a part of the peculiar people willing to stand for biblical principles no matter what the cost. Hostilities against Bible believing Christians will grow significantly. **Thus it is important to know what the Biblical worldview (values) are and why we are committed to them.**

JOHNNY COOPER

In 1965 we were attending a little Assemblies of God church in Forestville, Maryland, pastored by a Canadian, George LeRoy. George became a very good friend as he shepherded me and taught me the things of God. If God had not brought us together, it would have been very difficult to attend his church. While attending church you hoped nobody would recognize your car parked there: Sunday morning, Sunday evening, Wednesday night, and most Friday nights. But God frequented that little church, so we wanted to be there.

I came to know George in an interesting way. Your mother called me one day at the Senator's office and told me to expect a call from a Reverend George LeRoy. I soon received the call and he told me I was needed to help him (and another Christian brother, Romey Cutright) rescue the wife of a very prominent medical doctor. The story was compelling, so I agreed to help. They picked me up at the New Senate Office building and as the four of us

(George LeRoy, Romey Cutright, Bob Gardner and I) drove to Baltimore, I learned the details of the story.

Johnny Cooper was a woman in her mid-fifties who had received the baptism in the Holy Spirit, prayed in tongues, and quoted Bible scriptures. She had called George early that day and informed him there were doctors at her home that very moment, with an ambulance. They were going to administer an injection (with a needle!) to supposedly "calm her nerves," and take her to a private mental institution in Baltimore, the Sheppard Pratt Psychiatric Hospital. She explained the doctors had allowed her to make one phone call. She called George.

George sprang into action and called his friends Romey and Bob. They thought they needed a lawyer and called your mother to see if I would likely go. That was a big question.

I 'felt' compelled to go but was a bit leery in that I only knew Romey and he was more than peculiar – a real foot stomping Pentecostal. I was new to the experience. The terminology and behavior was not what I was accustomed to.

On the forty mile drive to Baltimore, we prayed with the little understanding we had and a lot in the Spirit. The three of them stayed in the car to pray when we got to Sheppard Pratt. I went in not knowing what to do or what to expect - and hoping I could get back out. I asked to see the administrator and was escorted to his office. I introduced myself and explained that I was the Legislative Assistant and Legal Counsel to a United States senator and was concerned for the well-being of a friend, Johnny Cooper.

I was taken upstairs to a very luxurious living room and instructed to wait for Johnny. I did not like being in the place. I was very nervous. I had never seen 'my friend' and she had never heard of me. And we were to meet in an insane asylum?

Soon a peculiar looking woman (with too much make-up and too big a smile) came straight for me and greeted me with a hug as she said her name was Johnny. I was not used to being hugged by a strange woman, particularly in an insane asylum.

I did not get a chance to ask any questions. She started talking. According to her story, her doctor husband was looking for a way 'to get rid of her' because of her Christian commitment. He was offended by the fact that she 'pled the blood' over his pillow and prayed in tongues as she moved around the house; that she left him scripture notes both on his dresser and on his mirror.

At that time these expressions and customs were more than strange. (Now I accept them because I have experienced them.) I didn't know how to get her out of the institution, and I wondered if I could get her out, would I be doing society a favor?

After about twenty minutes with Johnny, I returned to the three men left praying in the car. My first comment to them was a question. "I met with a woman fifty plus years of age, who had too much make-up, quoted scriptures excessively, claimed to have a husband who was a doctor who did not appreciate her 'pleading the blood' over his pillow or leaving scriptures around the house. Was that Johnny Cooper?"

They laughed and assured me she was indeed Johnny. Then in all seriousness I said, "I am not sure we are doing anyone a favor to try to get her out of this mental institution."

George, who knew her best, assured us she was okay and that she was taken there against her will. We did not know what else to do, so we made a fast-food stop and then headed home in the dark of the late evening.

Shortly after I was dropped off at our apartment at Pennbrooke Terrace on Silver Hill Road, George called to tell me that Johnny was already at her home in Washington, DC. She had been driven to her home before we could get back to ours. She was a little nervous about what her husband might do.

Johnny had learned and then shared with George, that when the Washington, DC, doctors took her to this private, exclusive and expensive, mental institution in Maryland, the admitting officials would not accept her. They needed sworn statements from two *Maryland* doctors who had examined her and had determined that she was mentally ill and needed treatment. The two District of Columbia doctors took her paperwork to two Maryland doctors and asked them to sign the necessary papers stating they had indeed examined Johnny Cooper and found her to need admission to Sheppard Pratt, when in fact, they had never seen her. Do doctors sometimes cover for doctors?

The Sheppard Pratt officials knew all this and were willing to go along with the plan. But when a lawyer with a title of Legislative Assistant and Legal Counsel to a United States senator came into the scene, Sheppard Pratt feared the rules of engagement had changed and they did not want to play in that game. She was loaded up in a very nice car and delivered to her home in Washington, DC.

I had done nothing it seemed. What was the reason I raced from the office to the Baltimore hospital? **Sometimes God just asks us to 'show up' and He will do the work.**

The following Saturday I went to see 'my friend' Johnny and to meet her husband and college-aged children. My purpose was to let the doctor know that Johnny had real friends, outside his circle of friends, who believed she was a sound and wonderful woman.

Apparently I followed my script very well because Johnny lived for many years after that traumatic event, winning souls for Jesus. In fact she led several of her own children to the Lord. Her eldest son became a medical doctor. After he received the Lord as Savior and the baptism in the Holy Spirit, he fully understood his mother and he and George became very good friends.

My Dad - 1983 (1907-1990)

MY DAD WAS FOR ME

Mom asked me to drive over to Westside Grocery to get a loaf of bread. I did so. On the way back, I crashed our Nash into another car at an intersection about four blocks from where we lived in an apartment in the downtown Globe Hotel in Wheatland, Wyoming.

As a small crowd of people started gathering around the wrecked cars, I went to a house and called my dad and reported what had happened. He said he would be 'right over.' As I waited for him, I listened to the conversations of those gathering and looking over the accident. Their talk was all about "these reckless teenagers." I wondered what was going to happen to me.

As I hung around the perimeter of the growing number of observers, I saw my dad just slowly walking toward us with his hands in his pockets. He was whistling! With his eyes he acknowledged my presence and walked, calmly dignified, right into the crowd. I heard him asking as he pointed to the other car, "Where is the driver of this car?" Then I could hear his voice quietly asking others to go and smell the breath of the other driver. Soon the conversations of the small crowd were about "these drunken drivers."

The police came and the wreckers hauled both cars away. As dad and I walked back to the Globe Hotel, he showed me understanding. He never accused me of speeding or reckless-ness. He knew I was suffering enough. **My dad was for me!**

Oh - and I was carrying the loaf of bread!

SISTER SIZEMORE

Many years ago while working in Washington as a lawyer for Wyoming's United States Senator, I had a dramatic experience and committed my life to Jesus Christ. Soon I was being shepherded by a wonderful minister who would take me on his 'calls.'

Sunday evening church was testimony time. I would jump up to tell of the miracles of God I had witnessed with Brother George, as he ministered to his flock. The congregation would erupt with praises and shouts of thanks to God. Then Sister Sizemore would stand and say, "Twenty-seven years ago I gave my heart to the Lord Jesus Christ and I thank God for His keeping power." As the next person would stand to give a testimony, I would mutter to myself, "If Sister Sizemore doesn't have anything more exciting than that to say, why does she waste our time?"

The next Sunday evening, I could be found jumping to my feet to share with the church how God had miraculously met the financial needs of a brother, or resolved a marriage problem of a couple, or healed a small child. With each such testimony, the members of the church would explode with praise and thanksgiving to God for the miracles experienced. And as sure as anything, ol' Sister Sizemore would stand and say, "Twenty-seven years ago I gave my heart to the Lord Jesus Christ and I thank God for His keeping power."

I would just shake my head. Why would she tell something seemingly so mundane.

Life for me was anything but mundane. We were given and raised two wonderful children. As the years unfolded, I would receive some great honors and gain significant achievements. Those were followed by painful experiences that tested the foundations of my faith. I found those foundations to be secure.

Under God's hand, I moved on through more successes and new crushing experiences. Life was never mundane or boring.

Through the course of my life, wonderful family and friends have committed to help me 'finish the race' strong. They have seen our testimony unfold. Sometimes it was necessary for your mother to "carry my stretcher." Sometimes I carried hers. Your mother has always faced her challenges with a great attitude. You, Erin and Terry and your children and you, Eric and Becky and your children, are experiencing the ups and downs of life but prospering in every meaningful way. We are very grateful to God and we are proud of each one of you.

As your mother and I move toward the victory tape at a slower pace, we are encouraged as we hear your testimonies (both the unusual and the ordinary are exciting) and as we watch you take every curve and jump every obstacle in the race set before you. You can count on continued stories God is writing in our lives, too. But the one you'll be hearing more frequently is borrowed from ol' Sister Sizemore: **"Thank God for His keeping power."** I owe the Lord an apology for all my grumbling and thanks to Sister Sizemore for her powerful testimony.

Our evening uniforms

FRIENDS OF ISRAEL

In June of 1982 with President Reagan's support, the Israeli military forces invaded Lebanon. But they kept on marching and invaded the capitol, Beirut. This was done without America's foreknowledge or approval. It 'just so happened' that at the same time, all of the Reagan Cabinet members and their wives had been listed as honorary hosts of a Bonds for Israel dinner in Washington, DC. The White House's secretary of the Cabinet called and personally advised me that neither the President nor the Vice President would be attending because of the invasion of the city of Beirut; nor would the Secretaries of State or Defense. I asked if I were being instructed not to go and was told, "No, we're just advising you that the President and Vice President are not going. We would never tell you what to do."

Your mother and I believe that **when your friends are under attack you should stand with them.** We determined to go.

As we walked into the banquet hall, there were surprised faces. It became obvious that we were the only members of the Reagan Cabinet in attendance. There were a few members of Congress, all of them Jewish, and a much smaller crowd than had been anticipated. Immediately we were escorted to meet the man who had just been named as Israel's Ambassador to the United States, Moshe Arens. As it turned out, this dinner was to be his formal introduction to the United States government officials.

Arens was born, raised, and educated in Brooklyn. He was well versed on all things American and what my responsibilities were at the Department of the Interior. He was keenly aware of the support evangelical/pentecostal Christians gave to Israel as distinguished from the mainline denominational churches. I can attest to these matters because those were the subjects we discussed during the formal dinner.

In the conversation, I explained how hard I was pushing to develop our energy resources onshore and offshore. And how necessary it was to reduce our dependency on Mid-East oil (Arab oil). I stated that we needed congressional support. Arens acted surprised that I was suggesting we did not have the congressional support we wanted. When Arens spoke to that issue, I brought into the conversation Senator

Rudy Boschwitz, a Minnesota Republican of Jewish decent, who had been listening (as had all the persons at our round table). I said, "Rudy doesn't even support our efforts." My comment highly offended and embarrassed the Senator. He responded, "I have never been opposed to your energy programs." To which I stated, "Rudy, you have never spoken in favor of them." Arens quickly moved in and gave a lengthy statement of support trying to offend no one. He was great.

The next week, I wrote a letter to the new ambassador telling him how much we had enjoyed our evening. I also stated that if America was not successful with our energy development, we would not be able to meet our obligations under The Camp David Accord - which required America to guarantee that Israel was supplied with adequate energy.

I made that letter available to the press. The subject matter blew sky high when a liberal rabbi from New York City attacked me vigorously for supposedly threatening Jewish interests. It 'just so happened' I was previously scheduled for a speaking engagement with B'nai B'rith in New York City the week after the *New York Times* article. I don't believe in coincidences, by the way.

As I was driven up to the B'nai B'rith building, I was surprised to see the security force surrounding the area and to learn of the intense security measures the Jewish have to make for the safety of their members in organizations like the B'nai B'rith of New York City. After going through their security apparatus, I entered a large, packed ballroom set up for the luncheon, with press personnel stuck in every available spot. I was graciously introduced to this packed-out crowd.

Knowing how the traditional politician would address such a crowd, I chose to do it my way. With no salutation or warm greetings, I said, "I am a man of faith. I believe that Jesus Christ is the Messiah." And then I proceeded to outline our national energy needs and threats and what we had to do to address them. I took questions from the crowd. I received a powerful ovation and thanks. And even the press was good after that presentation.

With the encouragement of the White House staff, a new friend by the name of Fred Balitzer, set up a tour of synagogues and temples for me to address in Florida and California. The reception your mother and I had was tremendous. We enjoyed the people immensely. I cannot know for sure and thus I can not prove anything, but I will always believe that in our tour of the American Jewish communities, our reception was beyond warm and gracious because Ambassador Moshe Arens sent the word out that **we stood as friends of Israel.**

THE JERICHO MARCH

We became very good friends with our pastor George and his wife Ruth, in part because of the issues discussed in my story on Sister Sizemore and several other stories.

For an extended period of time, Ruth was sick and not able to function in the church or at home. In those days we addressed each other as Sister LeRoy and Brother Watt. It was not until we had been in the church for about two years that I asked a group of my church friends, as we men stood around talking, "Do any of you have first names?" They laughed and we started addressing one another as Brother Jim, Brother Nick, Sister Ruth, etc. It was not until years later that we used just the first names.

George was very intense in his ministry on the question of healing. He believed no one should ever die from an illness or sickness. So it became a real issue for him and the church that his wife, Ruth, was sick for these several weeks. We checked to see if there was 'sin in the camp,' rebuked the devil, fasted and prayed, quoted scripture, shouted, claimed the victory, and everything else we had heard Oral Roberts, Derek Prince, Charles Simpson, Bob Mumford, or Romey Cutright do. Nothing brought a healing to Ruth.

In the spring of that year, your mother received direction from the Lord on how healing was to come to Ruth. She believed God had told her four of us were to go that evening to the parsonage, march around their house seven times praying in tongues, and claim the healing. She thought it was to be Romey, Bob, herself and me. She of course was nervous about whether or not I would do it. But believing she had heard from God, your mother called the other men to see if they could make it to our apartment by the time I got home from work. They both agreed to meet at our place at 6:30 P.M. Everyone assumed I would get home on time and the men presumed I would be willing to go.

When I got home, Bob was already there. I did not like the sounds of the proposal and was delighted when we received a phone call from Romey saying he could not make it. Your mother did not know what to do. She was confident she had heard from God that four, not three, were to walk around the house seven times. At that moment an unexpected knock was heard at our apartment door. I opened it and there stood Brother George. He said, "What is going on here? God told me to stop by on my way home."

Your mother jumped with joy. George was the fourth member of the team.

She explained to George what God had instructed her to do and that she believed he was the fourth man. He said he 'felt the witness' to that. There was no way out for me. We loaded up and headed out.

When we got to the parsonage, we started walking around the house praising God and praying in tongues – out loud. Seven times we walked around that house; all of us soaking wet from the rain. I was delighted that it was raining the entire time. That reduced the possibility some neighbor might see us waving our arms and praising God in an unknown tongue as we walked those seven laps.

Ruth heard the commotion and quickly figured out what was going on. We entered the house after the seventh circling, laid hands on her, asked God to heal her, and claimed the victory.

Ruth was instantly made well.

It was a learning experience for me. God does take care of us. **We are to listen for His voice. We are to act in obedience to what we think we hear from God. He will honor that faithfulness – even if it looks foolish.**

Cabinet meeting has not begun, staff is busy.

DO NOT ACCELERATE THE PLANS OF GOD

Brother George was great at getting inter-esting speakers to come to our 'dumpy' little church. Being in a suburb of Washington, DC, and near Andrews Air Force Base, I sus-pect the speakers were motivated to some degree to come to our church so they could later tell audiences, "When I was preaching in Washington, DC, the nation's capitol, I said …" In any event, he had some very interesting and talented men of God speaking to us.

One of the impressive speakers was a Canadian by the name of Willard Cantelon. He spoke on the "Mark of the Beast," "The One World Government," and a "World-Wide Currency for the End Times." I was totally enthralled with him and his presentation. He was an excellent speaker and knew more facts and numbers than anybody I had ever heard speak. I just took it all in.

The second year he came and gave the same exact sermons. I took notes furiously. He was very good.

The third year he came and gave the same exact sermons I had heard twice before.

I never heard of or saw him for the next twelve or fifteen years. But a lot had happened in my life to move me beyond the Potomac and the Forestville Assemblies of God, out to the Rocky Mountains and back again, to Washington, DC.

In February of 1981 I went to the White House for a Cabinet meeting. Marty Andersen, the President's scholar and advisor (and a guy I really liked) called me aside. He told me that on the agenda was an issue being promoted by the Attorney General, William French Smith. Bill wanted to get the President to sign off on comprehensive immigration legislation being pushed by Senator Alan Simpson, my Wyoming Senator.

I looked at Marty with a blank stare. What did that have to do with me, the Secretary of the Interior? I was in charge of skunks and coyotes on the public lands.

He said something to the effect, "This bill calls for a universal identification card. We cannot let the President be put in a position of supporting anything that looks like the 'mark of the Beast.' I let him know that I agreed with him but asked why he was asking me to get involved. Since White House staff members were not allowed to speak at Cabinet meetings unless called upon, Marty explained, "You are the only one at the table who understands the real issue."

The President called the Cabinet meeting to order and proceeded with the agenda. Soon he was introducing the Attorney General and asked Bill to brief the Cabinet on the comprehensive immigration legislation. The Attorney General made a fine presentation which raised no issues that would concern anyone. It sounded okay to everyone, including me.

The President then turned in his chair and looked at me, sitting two chairs from him, (the Secretary of State, Al Haig, was between us) and said, "Jim, do you have any comments or concerns?" Obviously, Marty had told him I would be intervening on the matter.

With a little bit of alarm, I looked over at Marty sitting directly behind the President. His eyes said very clearly, "Jim, now is the time to speak up and protect the President – or else."

I stammered a bit, and said, "Mr. President, I have some very serious concerns about this bill. I think rather than take your time, I should discuss the matter with the Attorney General. We can then bring it back to you and the Cabinet for discussion."

The President said that was a good idea and moved on to the next agenda item. I did not know exactly what to do with the Attorney General - so I did nothing. I never called him, nor did he call me. A couple of weeks passed and I saw that Bill had put the immigration issue back on the agenda for discussion at the upcoming Cabinet meeting.

Again the President asked the Attorney General to present the issues of concern in the legislation and why it was needed. He did a very good job. The President then turned to me and asked if I had worked out my differences with Bill. I told him I had not met with the Attorney General to discuss the issues. He was very kind and did not seem to be disturbed about the matter at all. However, Bill Smith showed some irritation. I just smiled and nodded at him.

Another two or three weeks passed and the immigration legislation was again on the agenda for the Cabinet meeting. Of course, neither the Attorney General nor I had made any effort to discuss the issue. I do not know why he did not call me and push the point. I did not call him because I did not know what to say.

One morning I was under pressure because at that day's Cabinet meeting, we were to not only discuss but resolve the immigration issue. As I was leaving for the office at my usual time (7:30 A.M.), I asked your mother if she could find Willard Cantelon before I went to the White House.

Your mother is a good little detective. Somehow she was successful in tracking him down at the JFK Airport in New York City, getting ready to board a flight to Brussels where he headed up a Bible College for the Assemblies of God. She gave him instructions on how to get me by phone and called me to clear the lines for him.

When the phone rang I said, "Willard?" The last time I had spoken to him twelve or fifteen years earlier, I had addressed him as Brother Cantelon.

I explained to him that in a few minutes I would be leaving for the White House to attend a 10 A.M. Cabinet meeting. A meeting to discuss the immigration legislation that called for a universal identification card similar to what he had taught about as the 'mark of the Beast.' And I asked him what he thought I should do.

He started giving me one of the sermons I had heard years ago. I cut him off. Again I said I needed ideas on how to handle the matter. He started giving me another sermon. I raised my voice and shouted in an effort to cut off the sermon he had given a gazillion times and I had heard three times before.

I said, "Willard, the Cabinet meetings starts in less than 10 minutes. I am going to slam this phone down and go. I cannot be late to a meeting with the President. Do you have anything that would help me on this matter?"

Willard Cantelon was silent.

And then, as your mother would say, a holy moment came on the phone. I heard Willard Cantelon almost whisper, **"Do not accelerate the plans of God nor obstruct the plans of God."**

I quietly said, "Thank you, Willard," and gently laid the phone in its receiver.

I strode to my chair just moments before the President came into the Cabinet room. After he took his seat, we all sat down and the meeting commenced with the Attorney General making his presentation on the legislation dealing with the complicated immigration problems. As he finished, everyone in the room looked at me and the President said, "Jim, would you give your arguments?"

My eyes locked on the President's. Realizing I had heard from God through Willard, I said, "Mr. President, I have nothing to say."

The President's eyes registered both surprise and wonderment. Marty Andersen quickly spoke to Ed Meese, a senior staff man to the President and later Attorney General. Breaking the protocol and in a loud authoritative voice, Ed said, "Mr. President, I suggest you take it under advisement."

The President immediately turned to the next item on the agenda. No one ever again mentioned the matter to me, nor did the issue of a universal identification card ever again come to the desk of President Reagan.

There are some things we are to do. There are other things that we are not to do. But in all things we should remember: **Do not accelerate the plans of God nor obstruct the plans of God.**

LEARNING FROM THE LEFT

S ome time in 2002 or very early in 2003, I was contacted by someone at The Center of the American West, University of Colorado at Boulder, and was asked to join a conference they were going to sponsor called something like "A Conversation with the Secretaries of the Interior." The Executive Director, Patty Limerick, explained her plan to have all the living men who had served as Secretary of the Interior share a stage and discuss their roles managing the majority of the lands of the western states. The Department of the Interior is the dominant landlord of the West.

Patty explained how important it was for me to be there because I had made some of the greatest changes in the policies of the Department. And furthermore the other two Reagan Secretaries of the Interior had already declined because of "scheduling conflicts," even though the date had never been set.

I told this charming but forceful woman (whom I had apparently met some years before) that my calendar was wide open but there was no way I would accept an invitation to come to Colorado University for a meeting of any kind. I explained I considered CU a communist cell and was not willing to subject myself to their abuse. (Some issues and some people are impossible to deal with. You have to take control of the situation. Not easy to do.)

Patty liked my open candor and responded in kind. As succeeding phone calls came, I made suggestions on how I thought the proposed program could be shaped, formatted, and developed. To my surprise, Patty accepted my suggestions even though they were always followed by my comment that I would never participate in a CU event. The students and particularly the faculty had a very bad reputation among my conservative community because of the rude and crude reception the university had given those conservatives who had accepted invitations to their campus.

As Patty and I discussed a newly proposed idea, (that each living Secretary should be invited for a different month) I would give her my views and my perspective on those who had served the Department and their respective presidents. I knew all of them professionally or personally except for Cecil Andrus. For example, I had been a young lawyer serving a Wyoming senator when Stewart Udall was

Secretary. I watched during those four years how Udall handled my hostile senator and admired how he did it. I had great respect and admiration for him and determined to follow his examples – I tried to learn from all those who did well.

During this planning process I grew to respect and trust Patty. In fact she won my friendship. I liked her. She was trustworthy and 'coachable' and I always learned something in the many conversations we had. I agreed to go to Boulder in February of 2004. It turned out to be a great experience for me and I trust for The Center of the American West and the University of Colorado.

My visit to the campus produced all the predictable events: an aggressive press; an ambitious university president wanting to be seen with a *real* conservative so that she could use the event to show how fair she and the university were; a know-it-all Sierra Club-paid official; a cheap-shot by the local United States congressman; a wonderful turnout; splendid times with the faculty and students; a warm reception by the many supporters of the Center; and most of all, an enhanced friendship with Patty and Jeff Limerick.

Patty managed all dimensions of every aspect of the many events: fundraisers, long, taped interviews for historical study, National Public Radio and the press, faculty sessions, meetings with the students, dinners, the university president, and the main event.

Later when Stewart Udall was on the CU campus as a former Secretary of the Interior, Patty told him of the high regard I had for him. He was of course flattered and pleased. In fact Patty tried to get us on the phone together while he was in Boulder.

She was great.

The wonderful friendship continued with Patty after my February 2004 visit to the CU campus.

On Tuesday August 9, 2005, I had an early breakfast meeting, followed by an 8:30 A.M. breakfast at the Wort Hotel in my home town of Jackson. I arrived and found a table for two. I was meeting the just-resigned Deputy Secretary of the Interior, Steve Griles. He had been one of my closest advisors when I served in Interior.

I noticed a table of five or six people who kept looking my way - they were obviously talking about me. Jerry Spence was the only one I recognized. In addition to Jerry, there was a woman, two or three men, plus an older man – and I was sixty-seven, at the time.

About forty minutes into my breakfast, I watched as the group from that other table headed my way. I tensed up. Spence never wants anyone in the room who might detract from his presence. I did not want trouble (another interesting story behind that thought).

One of the men said, "Do you recognize who we have here?" No one likes that question; it embarrasses all concerned. I looked into the eyes of the old gentleman and had no idea who it was. The elderly man, having a stage presence, quickly introduced himself, "Stu Udall."

With delight and eagerness, I reached out to shake hands with the respected warrior of past conflicts. He reached up and pulled me down to hug me. I was shocked - and pleased. I quickly said, "We have a common friend who is your cheerleader and a great admirer, Patty Limerick."

With the grace of a seasoned performer, he stepped back from the hug and addressed the little group of now seven or eight. "Patty told me you said you admired me."

"I told her more than that; I told Patty that not only did I admire and respect you, but that I had tried to pattern some of my behavior after you. You handled my senator so well."

Looking straight at Jerry Spence I said, "Milward Simpson had a great distrust for the National Park Service and took it out personally on Secretary Udall. The Secretary always handled Milward with dignity and class. I knew I wanted to handle difficult people the way Secretary Udall handled Milward."

With that, all the parties were introduced around and the impromptu meeting broke up.

It was wonderful that Patty had laid the ground work so that Stu Udall might have the opportunity to receive an expression of my feelings and respect for him - a leader of the 1960s. Stu Udall was a distinguished man of the opposite political party who had modeled for me (back then I was a twenty-five year old lawyer) a behavior that I wanted to emulate.

I did not get the chance to tell the former Secretary the other things I had said about him in my presentation to The Center of the American West at CU. The CU campus faculty and students are for the most part 'greenies.' Udall is thought to be 'Mr. Green,' so I had expressed to the evening crowd my disappointment in the fact that while I set many records when serving as Secretary, "I did not come close to Secretary Udall's records of drilling wells, mining lands, digging ditches, or damming rivers. But I tried."

I have been privileged to observe men and women of different persuasions perform in a variety of situations. **You can learn something from people even though you do not agree with them.**

THE SEVENTH MENTIONING

My friend Steve Shipley and I were meeting with Reverend Jerry Falwell's key man in Washington, Cal Thomas, on some important matter.

Steve, my trusted aide of many years, complained to Cal that he had been trying to get me to do something he thought needed to be done.

Cal responded with a question, "Have you applied the *law of the seventh mentioning*?" Both Steve and I drew a total blank.

Cal then explained that when he wanted Jerry (Falwell) to do something, he would recommend it, knowing full well the suggestion would be rejected or ignored. In a few days Cal would bring it up again. After a few more days the subject matter would again be brought to Jerry's attention. Again and again. About the fifth time Cal mentioned the subject, Jerry would inevitably say, "I have been thinking along those lines." On the sixth mentioning, Jerry would say something like, "Remember I shared that with you the other day. I am glad you like my idea."

On the seventh mentioning, Jerry would claim, "I have had this idea and I have given it a lot of thought. I want you to implement my plan of action. I know it is right."

Cal would finally get to do what some days before he had thought was right.

The law of the seventh mentioning is very powerful in the work place, in the church, and in the marriage. I have used it. (And it has been used on me!)

I was privileged.

REAGAN'S KINDNESS

When I was called to Washington to inter-view Governor/President-elect Reagan, I was prepared to discuss six areas of major change he had promised to bring about if he was elected. I was well versed and experi-enced in the subject matters and surprised for a moment at his depth of understanding. But of course, for eight years as Governor of California, he had had to deal with the Department of the Interior that manages 50% of the lands of that state and all of the outer continental shelf of the Pacific Ocean. In that interview, I felt there was a strong meeting of the minds and a good ability for the two of us to communicate effectively. After he asked me to join his administration and I accepted, I said something to the effect: "What needs to be done will be very controversial and you will have to back me, and back me, and back me, and then fire me." We both laughed. With that characteristic twinkle he said, "I will."

Being Reagan's first Secretary of the Interior proved to be more controversial than I thought it would be. When a particularly bad story would appear in *The Washington Post*, I would receive a phone call from Ed Meese or Bill Clark (who at that time was the President's personal assistant and National Security advisor) who would say some variation of, "I just have been with the President and he wanted me to tell you to hang in there and not back down." Those phone calls were very valuable to me.

In the early years of the administration, Reagan called frequent meetings of the Cabinet. When we were seated, only the Secretary of State's chair separated my chair from the President's. Always, the President made a special comment to me or made a special eye contact. So much so that his personal staff began to ask me to bring up at the Cabinet meetings certain matters foreign to the interests of the Department of the Interior. Fellow Cabinet members sought me out to speak up on matters of importance to them. After conversation with other Cabinet officers, I began to realize that the President had established with me an unusually warm relationship.

While serving the President, I sometimes felt battle-weary and bruised, but I always felt privileged and in fact, favored.

A few weeks after I 'executed' myself from the Cabinet, the President made a Saturday morning radio address about my service to the nation. I had not heard it, nor had I paid any attention to it when it was mailed to me. I was depressed, discouraged, and so burned out that I never listened to TV or radio, or read a newspaper. I did not - could not - focus on what the Reagan administration was doing. It was a struggle to put my new life together.

However (skipping forward about thirty years) Perry Pendley, a personal friend and key member of our Department of the Interior team, attended the second Bald Eagle Reunion. After thirty-one years, my political appointees (The Monday Morning Group) met and there among other things, encouraged Perry to write a book specifically about our years together serving President Reagan at the Department of the Interior. The book is titled *Sagebrush Rebel: Reagan's Battle with Environmental Extremists and Why It Matters Today*, published by Regnery Publishing.

In doing his research, Perry caused me to focus on the President's radio address of November 26, 1983; and in doing so, I was honored and blessed by the fact that he said anything at all about me but particularly by what he said. The President, President Reagan, in his own personal handwriting, on a legal

**A portion of President Reagan's
handwritten radio address.**

pad, wrote out the radio address he would then give.

In a request for information, Perry wrote to one of President Reagan's speech writers, Peter Robinson: *"On October 9, 1983, President Reagan's diary notes that Jim Watt called from California and resigned as DOI Secretary. On October 19, his diary notes that 'Jim Watt came by [and] gave me a report on his stewardship & it reveals the hypocrisy of the Environmental lynch mob.' On Saturday, November 26, President Reagan devoted his radio address to Jim Watt's record; ... My question is who would have written President Reagan's radio address? Is there a way to find out? It sure sounds like him but I imagine a great speech writer could write in the style of the boss."*

Peter Robinson wrote back to Perry with the following, *"As it happens, I recall that radio address well. Why? Because the speechwriting shop had already composed an address—I don't recall the subject, although it may have been the economy. The President sent back our address with a couple of pages from a legal pad on which he had composed his own, the tribute to Sec. Watt. The President included a warm note, explaining that he hoped we speechwriters wouldn't mind if he set aside our draft for his own. We all marveled at his draft. He had composed it, single-spaced, with scarcely more than a word or two crossed out and re-written. He had simply sat down with a pen in his hand and written what he had wanted to say. Beautiful."*

In the turmoil of my resignation, President Reagan seized the opportunity not only to affirm one last time our relationship and what he and I had agreed was my role at the Department of the Interior, but he also used the moment to look ahead to the future of our nation. **In times of trouble, affirm where you can and find ways to move forward.**

I have included in the Appendix verbatim the full printed text of the President's radio address from the transcript of the official White House press release, November 26, 1983. It was sent to me years ago by Marlin Fitzwater, Assistant to the President for Press Relations.

ENCOURAGING OTHERS

After 'executing' myself from government, I signed up with a New York speakers bureau which sent me to many universities and business organizations to give speeches. It was very lucrative and took little if any preparation in that I had been sharpening my speaking skills with intensity during my Cabinet years. I would get on the plane, fly to the appointed destination, put on a positive face, and move with a great deal of confidence. Even so, inside I was burned out and exhausted from the stress that I had once relished while serving the President.

In one such instance, I had flown to Los Angeles to give a speech. The next morning, I went to breakfast with a friend. As we were eating breakfast, he told me to look at the editorial page of his *Los Angeles Times*. I told him I was not interested and furthermore I told him what I thought of the *LA Times.* (There was nothing good to be said about it.) He insisted and handed me the newspaper, opened to the editorial cartoon. I glanced down and saw their large political cartoon with the words, "Watt Lives - U.S. Supreme Court." My spirits soared and I was encouraged. Watt lives. I even smiled at the *Los Angeles Times*.

I have learned that we all need encouragement. I make it my practice to affirm and encourage my friends.

The footnote on this story is that every major change we at the Department of the Interior brought to the resource management of our natural resources was challenged by the environmental leftists. We won almost all of them at the federal district court level. A few were appealed and I have been told that nine of the legal contests went to the United States Supreme Court where we won them all. This case (the subject of the Conrad cartoon Watt Lives) was one of the more major challenges to the entire opportunity of finding oil on America's outer continental shelf. Jerry Brown, the then Governor of California, other leftists and environmental groups, challenged us clear up to the U.S. Supreme Court. And again we prevailed.

THE MONDAY MORNING GROUP

During my Cabinet years, our Department of the Interior political team was fiercely loyal and dedicated. Early on Monday of each week about fifty men and women, those I had politically appointed and approved, would gather to review the schedule of activities for the week. It was called The Monday Morning Group.

I always came prepared to leave them with a 'nugget' of political direction and motivation. We did not discuss substantive issues at that meeting, only schedules and plans for the week. The raw politics of procedures were discussed and labels and statements made that were not 'politically correct' or in some instances, not even nice. But the phrases and words did express our feelings about our Democrat opponents and the 'greenies'.

After one of those Monday morning meetings, I walked out with Steve Shipley, my chief of staff, who had been a faithful friend for fourteen years through five different jobs.

I turned to him and said, "Steve, this is the most talented and unusual group of men and women imaginable. Not one of them smokes or swears." Steve rolled his eyes as he shook his head with amazement at my naivety (or maybe stupidity) and said, "Jim, that is so only in your presence. **A leader sets the example.** You're their leader."

Never once was there an inappropriate leak to the press about what was said. Their loyalty was unmeasurable. No one was allowed to keep a journal, keep notes, or schedule logs. We had a 'clean desk' policy. But all were assured that when they left government, they could claim to have done anything they wanted to claim and we would back them up.

It was agreed that we would meet in twenty-five years. We did so in July of 2006 at the Jackson Lake Lodge in Grand Teton National Park. The bonded friendships were rich and rewarding. Again in 2012 they wanted to meet in Jackson Hole, thirty-one years after we first joined together to serve President Reagan. Many stories were told (and many of them were true), but all were amazing as they reflected the commitment and devotion of a team dedicated to Reagan's Revolution.

In the Reagan years we reported to nineteen congressional committees and sub-committees with the majority of the members of those committees dedicated to making us fail;

or to demean, ridicule, and degrade us. This is why few business leaders can successfully run an agency of the United States government. They expect their 'boards of directors' to be supportive of their defined objectives. Not so in the political theater of Washington.

At this 2012 reunion, I told of the friction that had built up between Congressman Morris Udall, the chairman of our major congressional committee and me, unlike my relationship with his older brother, Stewart, the former Secretary of the Interior. Mo and I met and worked out our differences. He agreed to do certain things, as did I.

Within a few days, *The Washington Post* ran a front page story telling how Chairman Udall had personally attacked me for doing something that was the subject of our earlier informal meeting.

I was furious. I grabbed the phone and called his personal office. His secretary told me that he was tied up in staff meetings and would be for a couple of hours. Knowing where Udall was, I told Stan Hulett, the head of our Congressional Affairs, to meet me in the garage. Now my personal security per-sonnel were scrambling. They had to notify the Capitol Hill police that we were coming and coming right now. They wheeled their cars out and we were on our way.

I walked into Udall's office with two huge men from my personal security squad right behind me. I said nothing to the secretarial staff sitting in the outer office and barged through the door of the Congressman's private office. Everyone in the room was more than startled. I barked out the order, "Staff, get out!" They scurried out like rats.

Now with just Stan and me in his office, the Congressman stood up. He was taller than I and probably twenty years older. Our eyes locked on each other and he said, "I lied."

I kept looking at him for what seemed like a long time, but probably only a few moments. Without saying a single word, I then turned and walked out of Chairman Mo Udall's office.

From that day forward the Chairman and I had a very professional relationship. It would probably be labeled a frigid one but professional, with full respect being given one to the other.

This was the type of story The Monday Morning Group shared at both the twenty-fifth and thirty-first anniversaries. They are outstanding, talented men and women who labored for their country and who worked as a team with immeasurable loyalty to me as their leader.

WHO RULED THE ROOST?

In 1969 I met a man by the name of Roger Ernst, a lobbyist for Arizona Public Service. Roger had served as Assistant Secretary of the Department of the Interior during the Eisenhower administration. He became a good friend and counselor to me when I served in the Nixon administration.

Roger came to see me, probably in late 1982, and after an extended conversation between two friends he said, "What did David tell you?"

I responded with, "David who?"

"You know, what did David have to say about energy?"

"I don't know who or what you are talking about."

Roger replied, "What did David Rockefeller tell you about energy?"

And I said, "I have never met David Rockefeller."

Roger jumped to his feet, stuck his hand across my desk and with gusto said,

"Congratulations, you are the first Secretary of the Interior, since the Eisenhower years, who has not taken his marching orders from David Rockefeller."

I realized once again that in serving the nation under President Reagan, we had the freedom to do what we knew to be right. I never felt an obligation to check it out with the 'Eastern Elite' or the 'Washington establishment.' I was accountable to the President, Ronald Reagan.

FRIENDSHIP

In reviewing my seventy-five years, I realize again that one of my greatest benefits has come from the accumulation of wonderful, talented, and interesting friends. In fact it has been a rich asset.

There are friends from the days in junior high, high school, college, the several tours of duty in Washington, Denver, Jackson, and now Wickenburg.

It would be foolhardy to try to list the friends, but heading up the list would be the one who I've been the closest to and the one who is the most important to me, your mother and grandmother. We became friends as thirteen year old junior high students and the friendship has only grown better and better. The other friends have come with all kinds of descriptions.

I have learned from each of them. They have broadened my outlook, taught me what they were interested in, tested me, encouraged me, and given me a helping hand at the right time. We have been able to learn, laugh, and love together. I have had great friends.

I have found that there are three types of friends: friends for the event, friends for the road, and friends for life.

A 'friend for the event' is a special relationship for a purpose. One of the reasons I have chosen to live in small communities is that it allows me to get to know a lot of interesting people. I know by name the postal clerks, the gals that work at the coffee shop, the clerks at the grocery store, the policeman, the waitress at the restaurant where our Bible study meets every Thursday, etc. They call me Jim and I greet them by their first names. We discuss the event, the weather, the football game and whatever the headline of the day might be. I do not know their spouse's names, nor where they are from, what their problems are, or their plans for the future. But we are good friends for the event.

A 'friend for the road' is the result of a deep commitment we make with others for an important cause. When I founded and ran the Mountain States Legal Foundation, I hired excellent lawyers and a superior staff to back them up. We challenged the liberal causes in the eleven Western states and established a remarkable record. I knew those lawyers and their spouses, their dreams and desires. We were warriors with a cause. They put their careers on the line for me and they knew I was doing the same for them. There was never a doubt about loyalty or devotion to the cause or the team members. They were great friends.

When my next 'assignment' came, to serve in President Reagan's Cabinet, I packed up four cardboard boxes full of clothes and records I thought I might need, got on a plane, and headed for Washington, DC. I never looked back. Those good 'friends for the road' and I do not even exchange Christmas cards. At one time we had committed our lives one to another; then suddenly we traveled separate roads.

A 'friend for life' is a unique relationship where you are so connected with the soul of the other person that nothing can separate your friendship: not time, distance, or other people. You stay in contact and when you get together, you pick up your conversation as if you had never been apart from one another. You celebrate one another's successes and suffer over each other's hurts - and you know which is which and when they are being experienced by your 'friend for life.'

THE UMBRELLA STORY

I had the same dream twice, within a few nights of each other. I didn't understand it and neither did your mother; but that didn't mean we treated it as unimportant. The dream didn't have a story line. It was a series of segments which we eventually called the *Umbrella Story,* even though there was no umbrella.

As the years unfolded, some of the meaning became clear and we passed that much on to you kids, thinking that the generations yet to come should walk under 'the umbrella.' I'm learning today that each of you has taken this story seriously. It has been formative in your expectation of God in your life and his favor upon you.

At the time of the dream in late 1963, we lived at Pennbrooke Terrace Apartments on Silver Hill Road. I did not know I was not a Christian. (My story of becoming a Christian is in the chapter "Do You Know Jesus?") The dream was enough of a puzzle to me to prompt your mother to invite Romey Cutright to our home. He was becoming a good friend and seemed to have an interest in this kind of thing, so maybe he could help me make sense of my vivid dream.

Although he wisely added nothing to my understanding that evening, Romey did convince me that God was talking to me and that I should pay attention. It took some years to understand what I knew.

In the dream I saw myself walking down a street in a downpour of rain, yet I remained completely dry. The fact that no rain fell on me, while others were soaking wet, led to the conclusion later that there must be an invisible umbrella present. Others on the street in the dream who were getting wet were asking one another, "Whose boy is that?" In other words, we are wet and he is dry. The answer that satisfied those in the dream but was a total mystery to me was: "Oh, that's one of Earle's boys." This was all very confusing because Earle was my uncle, not my father, and I barely knew him - but enough to know he was held in some mild contempt by my mother because his pentecostal religious views differed considerably from hers.

She was a Methodist with prejudice against people like the circuit riding Holiness preacher who in the early 1900s came into Powder River country, where the Watt family ranched. My grandparents and Earle took up with him and his teaching. My uncle Earle believed that this spiritual dimension was the most important part of his life. Why I was called Earle's boy in the dream took some time to understand.

The dream came in neat segments; none seemed to be related to the others except that I was a central figure. It was that first raining segment that bothered me back then.

The scene changed. In the dream I saw myself jumping from a balcony down to another balcony and to another. I did so over and over without any concern or fear; almost carelessly and without any effort.

The scene changed again to a large sports stadium with stairs going up between rows of chairs in the seating sections. I ran up and down those stairs repeatedly for no apparent purpose but I never got tired or winded or needed to stop.

Suddenly I was inside a rustic cabin where Uncle Earle lived on the Watt ranch in Powder River country, northern Wyoming. It was sparsely furnished and there was no food on the table - even though it was set with forks and plates for a meal. Earle invited me to sit down at the table and as we were seated, food came out of nowhere on to serving dishes. As one piece of chicken was taken from the platter, another one would take its place. There seemed to be no end of the food supply.

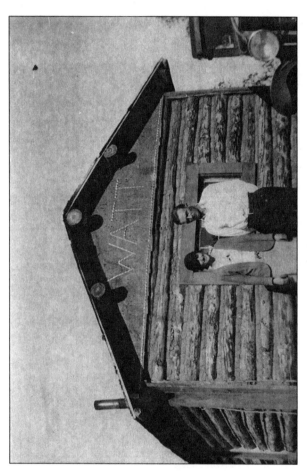

The homestead - 1930

The next scene was Uncle Earle insisting that we were to go outside. The reason is no longer clear to me, but I do remember that in the dream there was a raging, winter snow storm outside. I had no coat or hat and was concerned that it would be too cold and that walking in the storm would be foolish and impossible. The snow was blocking the exit and packed higher than the windows and doors. No one could see a thing.

Uncle Earle insisted and explained that as he stepped out the door, a coat would come. In the dream I was skeptical. It happened to him just as he said it would: a coat wrapped around him in the process of stepping out the door. And the wall of snow gave way in front of him. I followed. As I opened the door, a coat wrapped around me, as well as a scarf and hat. I did nothing to put them on: they were put on me.

Uncle Earle was nowhere to be seen. He left no cleared pathway behind him and again the snow was over my head and in close to my face. Yet as I stepped through the door, the pathway cleared one step at a time. Only one step at a time. In the dream I did not know the destination, but I just kept walking.

That was the end of the dream. Both times.

The following February 1964, I was born again and made a personal commitment to live a life for Jesus Christ. Even after I experienced the baptism of the Holy Spirit and the pentecostal ways - the orthodoxy of the first believers - I did not credit the dream. Your mother never forgot the dream - she had taken notes on my sharing, and even though I often told the story through the years, the 'umbrella' was not something I could do anything about.

Instead in the years to follow, I just walked out life out in a manner that seemed to come naturally. I walked with the confidence that this was the right way to follow Christ. I was never embarrassed because of my faith or pentecostal ways. Maybe I had become like 'one of Earle's boys' after all. My parents, your grandfather and grandmother, watched my life with interest and soon followed in the same pathway Uncle Earle and I walked.

Looking back now on my full and exciting life, I can see that just the way I met life was noticeably different. When storms of controversy were all around, my roots did matter. I was kept dry, so to speak. Covered from above.

I was not afraid to take risks. No matter what the obstacles, the gaps of knowledge, or the cautions of others, I saw the outcomes as possible and 'leaped' from one to another, unscathed and unhurt.

There were times in my career when I had unbelievable stamina, both mental and physical, and the sticking power of purpose.

Always there was provision - a time of rejuvenation after being spent in long battles. Always enough energy-building opportunity with people at the table.

I had protection that came just at the moments I needed it to face the debilitating blasts. I trusted my gut and my intuition to step out where I could not see. I had to trust God for the destination. I moved along with some fear, I admit, and with some fascination into whatever hard stuff was put in front of me.

It could be that **this dream was meant to tell me and you kids to expect God to show up unexpectedly and to give us His favor.** When He asks us to do something, be willing to do whatever it takes to stay under the protecting umbrella of God's grace and let Him do His stuff. That's what matters.

FRIENDS AND ENEMIES

During my Cabinet years, I learned that frequently in politics and life in general, there is "an equal and opposite reaction to every force." Examples: support versus opposition, kindness versus resentment, or confrontation versus avoidance. The problem is that without real discipline, our minds focus and remain on the negative experiences rather than on the positive, good experiences we have.

Those in positions of leadership invite active friendships as well as negative reactions. Thus, we have those who support us and those who oppose us, friends and enemies. Be sure that you are attracting the right type of friends, the people you respect. Know them, protect them and affirm them. The enemies will take care of themselves. But be alert, and do not get confused about who you want to attract: who you want on your side. I was doing what the President wanted and was not seeking the approval of the *Washington Post* or the *New York Times,* or the 'Eastern elite.'

When Governor Reagan (President-elect Reagan) announced that he would appoint me to be his Secretary of the Interior, the shrill and hostile voices of the liberal community, including the environmental selfish interest groups, went on the attack. They had easy access to the mainstream media and put their fundraising machinery in high gear.

I had expected some opposition because, for the first time in America's history, the environmental community openly and publicly went to the White House to show their full support for the liberal President Carter and their opposition to Governor Reagan.

We were surprised, however, to see and experience how sustained and aggressive the hostility was toward the new President; toward me, toward our Interior policies and programs, and toward my religious commitments and beliefs. *The Washington Post, New York Times* and *Los Angles Times* hired full-time reporters to cover nothing but me personally and what we were doing at the Department of the Interior. The other newspapers and magazines, plus the three TV networks (in those days, there were no cable programs or internet blogs that would allow for some balance) made similar commitments, but not necessarily by hiring full time reporters.

The consequences were that we were featured almost everyday on page one or page three of the *Washington Post*, with similar treatment by the other papers. There were cover stories in *Time, Newsweek* (twice), *U.S News and World Report* and a host of lesser magazines. I appeared on *Meet the Press, Face the Nation, 60 Minutes* (NBC and CBS Sunday programs), and repeatedly on the morning shows, *Today and Good Morning America* (NBC and ABC) and on and on it went. We were trying to tell our story and support the President.

Some of the coverage was neutral, but most had a negative twist and some stories were down right brutal.

What caught me off guard and continued to surprise us through the years, was the tremendously positive response to all the negative press. Apparently I was saying what the true conservatives wanted to hear, and in many cases wanted to say, but did not have the forum I had been given. I became a hot commodity for the Republican Party. They wanted me to raise funds for them. I told them I was not willing to travel as much as they wanted unless they paid for your mother to travel with me. The government would not pay for her travel.

The Republican Party's response was a blank check to cover your mother's travel and hotel expenses wherever I went on Interior business, if I would allow them to plan a

Republican fundraising event in those locations. *The Wall Street Journal* reported in 1982 that I was the biggest fundraising tool in the GOP arsenal, other than the President himself.

I had honed my speaking skills by giving my Christian testimony at dozens of Full Gospel Business Men's Fellowship meetings in the 1960s and 70s and fundraising for the Mountain States Legal Foundation. My speeches reached the emotional concerns of the audiences. There were reactions. I knew no other way to speak.

I should have caught on to the "equal and opposite reaction to every force" much sooner than I did. Probably the first missed opportunity happened in February or March of 1981. I had ordered that there would be no out of town travel for any of our political appointees until we made the massive changes the President had promised. We were only going to tell what we had done, not what we were going to do. Thus my only public appearances had been at congressional hearings.

However, Senator John Heinz (R-PA - yes, ketchup) was asking me and the Secretaries of Defense and Treasury to speak to about three hundred Pennsylvanians (fat cats) whom he had invited to Washington to learn about the new administration. At that time I did not really know Casper Weinberger or Don Regan, so I decided to accept the invitation and go early - to learn what they were doing and to learn what was being expected of me.

The Senator gave glowing introductions to each of the Secretaries as they were brought up from the front row to speak. He had known each of the men for several years and they in fact were distinguished men of accomplishment. I was honored to serve with them. They in turn were received warmly. I could tell by watching the crowd that they were thrilled to be there to hear from the new appointees who were charged with huge responsibilities.

After the other Secretaries left, the Senator turned to me, invited me up and gave a cold introduction. He let the crowd know that he had not known me and was not sure what I was doing; nor was he sure that he supported everything that I was intending to do. I felt like walking out before I spoke a word, but I determined to gut it out. To my surprise, the crowd stood and clapped. They had not done this for the other two when they were introduced and the Senator was more stunned than I was. When I spoke I gave them real 'political red meat;' attacking the liberals with zeal, knowing full well that Heinz was a liberal Republican.

After my fifteen minute presentation, they stood - some on their chairs - cheering and yelling. I did not know what to do. It was so unexpected. But the Senator knew what to do. He came immediately to me, put his arm around me and faced the crowd with the biggest smile imaginable. After several minutes of holding me in front of the crowd, he calmed them and with the greatest show of pride said, "I knew you would like my friend Jim."

It took me several minutes to work my way through the crowd as I left the room, stunned and surprised. This crowd's response was the first encouragement or support I had received outside of a few close friends, the White House staff, and the Interior political appointees; that response and their words of support were an introduction to what we would receive in the months ahead.

I did not start traveling until September of 1981 when I went to Jackson Hole to speak to the Western Governors' Conference. To our shock, one hundred and twenty members of the press flew into Jackson to cover that event. I started traveling more to get our story out. Crowds and demonstrations for and against us were experienced in almost every place we went - Jackson, Denver, Phoenix, Salt Lake City, Albuquerque, Los Angeles, etc. The Republican politicians loved it because they could get attention from the mainstream media if they associated with Secretary Watt.

One time we were in Tucson, waiting to speak at what was then the biggest fundraising Republican banquet in Arizona history. As we watched the TV news, we saw a newsman telling about the big Republican event coming up and the anti-Watt demonstrations that had been created. As he was reporting, a college age kid went running by and the reporter reached out and pulled him back. On live TV the student was asked, "Why are you here?" He responded, "I don't know but they told me I had to be in place by 6:30." And he raced on.

We laughed with delight knowing that this University of Arizona student represented the depth of understanding of most of our opposition. But even at that, the criticism was hard to live with. The mind tends to focus on the negatives, even though we know we should not let that happen.

One time while in the Los Angeles area, I was called by a White House official and asked to substitute for the Vice President at a big speech he was scheduled to give in Los Angeles. I was honored to do so. I gave one of my stem winders and it was received with wild enthusiasm. There was a long line of admirers waiting to thank me. A Congressman from Michigan, Guy Vander Jagt, Chairman of the Republican Congressional Campaign Committee, and a long time political warrior, stood in line for well over forty-five minutes. When he grasped my hand and pumped it, he said with enthusiasm, "That was one of the five best speeches I have ever heard." A high compliment from him, but I have since wondered who the other four were.

That is how our minds play tricks on us. It takes discipline to keep focused on the mission. I want you kids to remember that if you take a position of leadership you will be criticized and attacked.

In the midst of being attacked it is difficult to remember that your actions may have challenged (threatened) special interests: the offended's financial interests, political philosophy, belief system, social standing, or comfort zone. Is this acceptable to you? If not, change course. If so, charge ahead with confidence.

We have to believe that at some point you will be rewarded for doing the right thing. It may be much later, but rewards will come.

A leader is identified by those who support him and those who oppose him, friends and enemies. Be proud of the names in both camps. Do not get the names or groups mixed up.

ADVERSITY AND BLESSING

The Washington years with President Reagan (1981-83) were exhilarating and thrilling in many ways, but also filled with adversity.

In 1996 we were visited in Jackson by Bill and Vonnette Bright, Washington friends and the founders of Campus Crusade for Christ. Bill had followed my career in the Reagan administration, specifically as it related to the adverse public outcry against me and ridicule of my Christianity. Several times when he was in Washington, DC, he had reached out to encourage me. He felt the sting of the criticism aimed at me.

I first met Bill at some evening banquet in Washington. As was frequently the case, people would come to our table and ask if they could pray for me. I accepted of course and after their discrete prayer, thanked them. But on this particular evening after I granted permission to pray, the man started praying an authoritative prayer: asking God to strike down those environmentalists, those enemies from the Left, and for God to protect me from those evil forces. I was stunned. I had never heard prayers like that. I immediately liked the man. When he finished, I stood up from my chair to shake hands and learned his name was Bill Bright.

I told him I had never heard such a prayer, but I liked it. He smiled and said, "Sometimes you have to bring them down before you can lift them up." An immediate friendship was established.

As we sat together in Jackson, I shared with him my fears and concerns. He laid his hand on my arm and quietly in a prophetic way, spoke words that put the past years and the future into the perspective of one who is confident of God: **"Jim, God has tested you with adversity and now He is going to test you with blessing."**

The adversity part I got. My character had been tried by difficult circumstances, but I had held on to God through it all. In reality this covered challenges to my reputation, my conduct in Washington, the criminal charges, my ability to make a living, family chronic health issues, and questions regarding my faith and loyalties.

I understood being tested for adversity meant: Would I trust God with my life and activities? I knew now that I could not measure my worth by meaningful work or activities. I was already engaged in the toughest task of my life - becoming a **human being** as God intended, not just a human doing, as I had been.

But Bill had said I would be tested with blessing. I did not understand that part, nor could I do anything about it. It apparently would mean I would receive an abundance of blessings over which I must be faithful. This had not happened yet, as I understood things.

In January 1997, looking for direction and the next step, we went to Kona, Hawaii, to attend a Youth With a Mission Discipleship Training School called Crossroads. It was structured for older people who thought they were at a decision point in their lives. It was an extremely important experience for both your mother and me. The Christian training and learning to worship God was invaluable.

It was there that one of the leaders spoke words of prophecy over me to the effect that "you will receive income from sources you are not now aware of." The words were strong in themselves, but also reaffirming those from Bill Bright.

I did not disbelieve those words; nor did I really focus on them because there was nothing I could do about the matter, anyway. One never knows when circumstances will turn into temptation for greed or lust or will become an opportunity for sharing and serving. The battle is always about who is in control, God or me. Consequently, I had to be alert.

Some years before, Don Hodel, a personal and political friend since 1969 (my first Undersecretary, Secretary of Energy and then successor at Interior) had asked me to assist with a Houston company he had helped to start with a Christian man by the name of Terry Looper. Because I was not good at setting fees for my services, I was relieved when Don instructed me not to try to set the fee for my consulting services "because Terry would be more generous with you than anything you might be bold enough to request." Don was right, Terry was.

A wonderful friendship with Terry grew out of that business opportunity. After several years of consulting and serving on a board of advisors, he gave me a chance to make an investment in his company, Texon.

Suddenly the Texon company grew and expanded in ways that had never been planned at its inception. And the result was that I started to see the fulfillment of God's earlier statement that had given me hope: "You will receive income from sources you are not now aware of." God began testing me again, this time with financial income beyond my greatest expectations.

As I write this, the test is still unfolding: Will I trust God when I have more than enough? I pray that I will respond with stewardship and generosity as God would want me to handle these financial blessings.

1994 With my mother Lois (1911-2010)

COURAGE

My mother was the dominant force in our family. She was a good woman and strict about teaching values to my two sisters and me. And she was a role model of thrift, hard work, and self-reliance.

Some of the things she taught were not true; but they were good for training us up. For example: She drilled it in: *Watt boys always tell the truth.* Thus I became a compulsive 'truth teller' - which got me in a lot of trouble because I frequently put truth above discretion. For instance, while it may be accurate and truthful to describe a big, fat, ugly man as a big, fat, ugly man, it does not have to be *said*. The Commandments of God instruct us not to lie. That does not mean I always had to *tell* the truth.

Mom and Dad were always in a teaching mode. We were not homeschooled, but we were schooled at home all the time. My parents were determined to give us as many experiences as you could get living in a small Wyoming town.

I was allowed to sit in on adult conversations, but never allowed to say anything. I observed and asked questions afterward.

Mom was the disciplinarian in our family. In fact, if one of my friends misbehaved (according to Watt rules) or said an inappropriate word in our yard, he was sent home. Mom and Dad were adamant that I use words and reason (not fists) to settle disputes.

Language was important to Dad. I was never allowed to say 'naughty' words, cuss words. I told my dad it was unfair that other kids could say bad things to me but I could not say anything back to them. Dad instructed me to look at them with a mean face and say, "You dangling participle," or "You split infinitive." Many kids went home crying because I called them that terrible thing, "a dangling participle." Dad had me practice phrases and sentences over and over so that in the heat of conflict, I would say what I intended. He taught me that unexpected words had power to disarm somebody's anger or divert their attention, and that I could stand up for myself by dramatizing words.

Mom instilled confidence in us in an unusual way. Mom taught us that everyone was equal and we believed her. She taught us that the way we treated others would be the way we would be treated. It never occurred to me that leaders would lie to me or be less than straightforward in discussion. Over and over again during my Washington years I was surprised, sometimes stunned, and often caught off guard, to have opposition leaders lie to me. (In Washington, unlike anywhere else in the world, it is not proper to call a person a liar when he is lying to you or about you. But to a Watt, one who lies is a liar.)

Mom's teaching that we were all equal allowed us to believe that we could do anything. In spite of my reading deficiencies, when Mom said, "everyone is equal, some just work harder," I believed her. I just had to study harder than the next guy. I disciplined my time and my mind to concentrate on what I *could* do. To take in information in a way that made sense to me. I learned to focus with great intensity to overcome some handicaps.

(However, Mom may have caught on that we are *not* all created equal after several years of my unproductive piano lessons!)

Because of my mom's determination to train us up with these ideas, I always had the confidence that with hard work and disciplined determination, I could battle through all obstacles to a successful result. I learned to apply this in other arenas.

Mom never said it took courage and I never thought it to be courageous. I just called it disciplined determination. When I faced severe opposition, my friends and supporters called my determination courage. My opponents called it arrogant. I later learned that what Mom taught us is a definition of **courage: to act in accordance with what one believes to be right, even if vigorously opposed.**

When I was serving President Reagan, news reporters seemed curious about my determination to keep driving ahead. About my ability to stay on the course the President wanted when the host of liberals were attacking so aggressively. Because my behavior was not consistent with the Washington norm, press reporters would frequently ask, "How do you want to be remembered?"

I would respond, **"I want to be remembered for having the courage to do what I think is right."** That's what my mother taught me. So when I later wrote a book for Simon & Schuster I titled it *The Courage of a Conservative*.

I SAVED THE BEST TILL LAST

In May 2011 when I spoke at Eric's church, I began this way: For many years I have been coming to Virginia to be with Eric and Becky and the kids on Memorial Day weekend. As a good son, Eric has always invited me to speak and as a good father, I have always declined.

But this time Eric told of a conversation the church board had about the need for older - white haired - men who have walked with Christ to present testimony (and themselves) as role models. He told me Jim Parroco had specifically singled me out and said I should stand up and be a witness for the church.

That was a legitimate request because we are all role models, for good or bad, whether we like it or not. My testimony is one of the faithfulness of God, even when I have not been faithful. So I want to take the opportunity to share with you a few of the experiences of the Living Lord's direct involvement in my life.

(I had this whole speech for Eric's church loaded on my new iPad2. But I could not see it well nor could I control the screen; so I reverted back to my customary way of telling stories based on the outline in my head, having never been able to read well.

I told how after having had a dramatic experience of salvation, I came under the care of a young Assemblies of God preacher from Canada, George LeRoy, who had a powerful influence on my spiritual growth. I told how he took me on house calls and how I would report back to the congregation on the exciting things God had done, only to be annoyed by Sister Sizemore's bland and unchanging testimony, "Twenty-seven years ago I gave my heart to the Lord Jesus Christ and I thank God for His keeping power." You can read the chapter on Sister Sizemore elsewhere in the book.)

It was in those years that we were taught to expect to hear God speaking to us. Yes, by the scriptures; yes, by circumstances; yes, by others counseling us; but what I really mean and want to stress is: God wants to speak directly to us and He does speak to us concerning the ordinary affairs of our personal lives.

In our modern culture it is thought to be okay to pray - to talk to God. But you are suspect if you claim to hear God's voice in response. Hopefully, all of us are considered odd by the popular culture. Because each one of us should specifically be hearing directly from God.

We like to stress that Christianity is not a religion, but a relationship. If there is a relationship with Jesus, there must be communication - that means listening and talking, not just talking. He wants to talk to us but frequently we are so busy praying that we do not listen and, most often, are just too busy to hear when He is speaking.

Frequently Eric has called me from Virginia or Singapore or India or the Middle East to get confirmation of what he believes God is instructing him to do. He does not want my worldly advice, which I would be glad to give, or my counsel. He wants to know if he is correctly hearing from God. He always structures his question, not as a request for advice, but to get a yes or no answer. Such as, "Dad, I am dealing with a request that has been made of me. Ask God if I should or should not do it." There is no opportunity for understanding the issue, or sharing my experiences. He wants me to hear a yes or no from God to confirm what he thinks God is saying. Sometimes it is hard to know with certainty that we are hearing from God. We need confirmation.

With the request made on the phone by Eric, I do not ask for time to pray about it or to think about it. Eric expects God to speak to me right then, as do I. That is what Eric's mother and I taught him. While holding the phone receiver in my hand, I speak in an inaudible voice to God and He responds with an inaudible voice.

I then tell Eric what I think God is saying - yes or no. He usually responds, "Thanks Dad, I'll talk to you later," and hangs up. Leaving me to wonder what he is thinking. It may be days or weeks before he gives me an historical account of what was going on.

God wants to be involved as a communicator in our daily lives. Let Him.

(After I shared with Eric's congregation about twenty minutes worth of the stories also found in this book, I finished it up with the following.)

Well, I have testified to the several experiences God has given me over the years. It is my determined purpose to keep on running the race that God has set before me and to finish strong.

It is not always easy.

The stress can be overpowering,

the temptations for power can be alluring,

the victories can be exhilarating,

the personal attacks damaging,

the family demands overwhelming,

and the personal needs consuming.

But in each test and each victory there has been a lesson to be learned that helped me prepare for the next go round.

Now I *understand* some of the things I thought I knew as a young man standing at the Capitol Hill bus stop fifty years ago. And one of the things I understand is that those meaningful and rich experiences that helped to form my character when I first became a follower of Jesus were supported by the repeated testimony of ol' Sister Sizemore. Yes, I've saved the best till last.

"Forty-nine years ago I gave my heart to the Lord Jesus Christ. Thank God for His keeping power."

BE THERE!

As you kids know, this is the way I sign off on my letters and emails to you family members and special friends. It summarizes the contract I have made with you, my family – children, grandchildren and great-grand children: *Erin* and Terry (Joel and his Jackie and their little John; Kara and her Peter and their little True; Ethan, Elliot and Trent) and *Eric* and Becky (Ian and Kiersti) and with the others who are yet to marry into and be born in this family.

I am promising you (or the person to whom I am writing or speaking) that I will live my life in accordance with God's directives so that I can claim the promises of eternal life with Him and be in heaven. Waiting for us there will be Laura, our families, and all those on whose shoulders we stand—including that circuit riding preacher who rode through Powder River Country in the early 1900s. I am asking you - or maybe pleading with you - to promise the same so that we together will BE THERE.

Proud of you –
Dad
Pa) Ames
Grand Dad

APPENDIX

Remarks made by Secretary of the Interior James G. Watt before the Reagan political appointees at Constitution Hall January 20, 1983

LET REAGAN BE REAGAN

Two years ago we started coming to Washington in order to bring change to the government. The change that we sought was personalized in Ronald Reagan.

We didn't come to Washington just to improve international relations - although we have done it.

We didn't come to Washington just to rearm America - although we are doing it.

We didn't come to Washington just to improve the management of our lands and natural resources - although we have done it.

We came calling for "A New Beginning." We came to bring a new direction. We came with an agenda - let no one be persuaded to the contrary. We have our agenda. We came to restore the greatness of America.

But the greatness of America cannot be restored without change. Unfortunately,

Let Reagan Be Reagan

This short speech, delivered by Secretary of the Interior, James G. Watt, received several interruptions and a standing ovation when it was delivered to over 2,000 political appointees in Constitutional Hall on January 20, 1983, at the Anniversary of the Reagan-Bush Inauguration. After reading this call to discipline, you will better understand the dedication that drives the Reagan revolution and the call to let Reagan be Reagan.

change never comes without conflict and controversy.

Are we willing to withstand the conflict and the controversy? Nothing of value ever comes without a price.

What is the price that needs to be paid to bring about the change needed to restore America's greatness?

Long, hard, thankless hours.

Harsh criticism—critical pressure groups—ridicule by political cartoons.

Endless hearings before Congressional committees.

Hostile reactions from one special interest group or another.

But let the nation know that those of us who have volunteered to join the Reagan Administration are willing to pay the price.

We will pay it in terms of personal exhaustion or public abuse. How much?

Whatever it takes.

The people of America must be asking "How?" How can we fill a room like this with men and women with such dedication and such determination?

The answer is that we came to the cause not with a mere preference, but with all-out commitment to do good in our efforts to increase our national security, improve the quality of life, and to create jobs.

Our commitment is to the fundamentals of America.

The battle in which we are engaged is really not over such things as just criminal justice or clear air or dairy support programs. The battle is over the form of government under which we and future generations will live. Will it be a government that recognizes the dignity of the individual, or will it be a government that puts the institutions of a centralized authority above the rights of individual persons?

As we look through the pages of history, we see a recurring event. We see in that history that there is a yearning from the heart of mankind - a yearning for the right to live and associate and work, to be free to govern ourselves, and to protect our nation. It is a yearning that flows from the heart like a stream of life. A yearning for political liberty.

And yet in those same pages of history, we find another recurring event. We see that it is government that seeks to limit and destroy our political liberty - the heavy hand of government. Whether you call that government a dictatorship, or a king, or a monarch, or czar, or the Gestapo - whatever you want to call it - it is the heavy hand of excessive government that abuses this political liberty.

Parallel to that call is a cry that also flows like a stream from the heart of mankind. It is the cry that calls for spiritual freedom. Freedom to worship God. The freedom to assemble with those of like precious faith - the freedom to commit our lives to a doctrine and a belief in the Supreme Being. This call for spiritual freedom flows from the heart as well.

These two streams of life - one calling for political liberty and one calling for spiritual freedom - have flowed through the ages. The history books are replete with the stories of successes and failures. But there is one glorious moment where these two streams have come together to form a mighty river called America.

And yet here in America the same enemies of political liberty and spiritual freedom continue to use government in an effort to snuff out the flow of life that comes from the heart in the search for real political liberty and spiritual freedom.

Last week, my wife and I were in Los Angeles and we stood hand-in-hand in the Simon Wiesenthal Holocaust Memorial Center. We saw the pictures on the wall portraying the unfolding of the history of the hatred and discrimination that swept across Europe in the 1930s, leading to the death and destruction of six million Jews.

On the wall of the Holocaust Memorial was a picture of one survivor of the death camps pointing with shame at the leaders of the world at that time. My mind was seared with the words under that picture. The words were these:

> Here is to the world that did not care—
> those who had ears but would not hear,
> those who had eyes but would not see,
> [those who had mouths but would not speak...].

In our battle for spiritual freedom and political liberty, let it never be said that any one of us did not hear, or that we did not see, or that we did not speak. We must gallantly defend those principles that are America.

Change must come if the greatness of America is to be restored. We must rearm America so that we can live in peace. We must rebuild America if we are to be prepared for the 21st Century. And we must control government if we are to improve the quality of life.

Change must come.

How will it come, how can we bring the change that is needed? As I pondered that question, from the depths of soul I felt these words "Let Reagan be Reagan... Let Reagan be Reagan."

Remarks prepared by James G. Watt for the
1983 General Council of the Assemblies of God
Anaheim, California, August 13, 1983

"... IN A TOWN NEARBY"

Thank you for the prayer support you have
given to my wife and me. We feel that
support and are grateful for it. The President
frequently requests the people of America to
pray for the nation's leaders because he, too,
bears witness to the sustaining power that
comes when the people of God pray. Thank you.

As Secretary of the Interior, I am responsible for the stewardship over one-third of
America's land mass—750 million acres. The
decisions we make are important for us now
and for the generations yet to come. As we
prepare for the 21st Century and beyond, we
are deeply concerned about the environment
and the management of our natural resources.
We have made major changes in the way our
natural resources are managed. As a result, I
am able to report that all the Federal lands are
in better condition and better managed than

they were when we inherited responsibility for them almost three years ago.

The national parks are now being restored—the national wildlife refuges are being improved and the coastal barriers, wetlands, forests, deserts, and mountains are now under good stewardship.

As important as these responsibilities are, there is yet a more basic battle, a more important responsibility in which I am involved. The real struggle, the real fight, is over the form of government under which we will live and the form of government we will pass on to those of the 21st Century. Will it be a government that recognizes the dignity of the individual? Or will it be a government that elevates the institutions of a centralized authority above the rights of individual persons?

As we look through the pages of history, we will see that men and women have been engaged in a struggle that comes from their hearts. That struggle is a yearning for the right to live and associate and work as we want—to be free to govern ourselves and to protect our neighbors. It is a yearning that flows from the heart like a stream of life—a stream of life crying out for political liberty.

Out of the same pages of history, we see that it is excessive government that seeks to limit and destroy our political liberty—whether it is government by a dictator, a monarch, a warlord, a czar, or the Gestapo.

Those same history books also tell us of another cry that comes from the heart—a cry that calls for the freedom to worship God, the freedom to assemble with those of like precious faith—the freedom to commit our lives to a doctrine and a belief in the one true God. This call for spiritual freedom also flows from the heart, like a stream of life.

Again, it is excessive government that seeks to oppress spiritual freedom, just as it oppresses political liberty.

These two streams of life—one calling for political liberty and one calling for spiritual freedom—have flowed through the ages. The history books are replete with the stories of successes and failures, but there is one glorious moment where these two streams have come together in the destiny that God provided. They have come together to form a mighty river called America. And yet here in America the same enemies of political liberty and spiritual freedom continue to use government in an effort to snuff out the flow of life from the hearts of men and women.

That is our battle today. It is a battle to enhance political liberty and spiritual freedom. It is a battle that will continue. It is a battle that will require us to be vigilant at all times. Freedom is not free.

One of the responsibilities I have as Secretary of the Interior is the privilege of caring for the Nation's memorials and monuments. In that capacity, I have become involved in the development of a United States Holocaust Living Memorial in Washington, DC. In December 1982, I was asked to swear in new members to the U.S. Holocaust Memorial Council.

In preparing for the ceremony, I read the briefing books which alerted me to the fact that many of those to be present at the luncheon were survivors of the Nazi death camps. But nothing prepared me to meet one who has survived the atrocity of man against man. I struggled with my emotions. Words failed me, as I shook hands with Dr. Elie Wiesel, Chairman of the U.S. Holocaust Memorial Council, and also a survivor. To explain the impact, my wife and I shared with him this story told by a visitor to an underground church behind the Iron Curtain.

A pastor was returning to his church after years of torture and deprivation in a Communist prison. When he entered the back of the room, the singing stopped. None would have questioned the silence, for his physical appearance was appalling—pitiful. With barely the strength to maneuver to the front, the pastor turned to face the crowd; the silence deepened. No one moved. In suffering sentences, he greeted his flock and shared how Christ had strengthen him, had enabled him to endure. He thanked them for their prayers.

Exhausted, the pastor concluded and painfully shuffled his way to the exit. The continued silence was embarrassing to the visitor. There had been no welcome. No sound. No applause. Yet all their faces were soaked with tears. At the appropriate time, the visitor asked why the congregation had not responded or even acknowledged the presence of the pastor. With tears continuing to flow, the hushed answer came, "What does one say in the presence of someone who has suffered so much?"

Dr. Wiesel nodded his understanding.

After the ceremony and the luncheon, Dr. Wiesel escorted us to the elevator. He was expressing his gratitude for the role the Department of the Interior was playing in providing a living memorial to the Holocaust. It seemed so little to do. In parting, I hesitated a moment longer as we shook hands and I admitted to Dr. Wiesel that I felt the impact of his survival deeply. Entering the elevator, I heard my wife say to him, "In the presence of one who has suffered so much, what can anyone say." I turned to see the tears in my wife's voice meet those in his eyes.

I was but a child when the atrocities of Hitler raged through Europe. The meeting with Dr. Wiesel and the purpose of the U.S. Holocaust

Memorial Council captured my interest. I started reading and thinking and reflecting on what was going on today in America and, in fact, in the free world.

The story of the Holocaust is frightening. While it was historically and socially unique, the forces that created the Holocaust still exist. Other minority groups could be the subject of an attack on their spiritual freedom and political liberty.

The story does not start with the criminal torture, abuse, and destruction of a people. But first with an attack on the moral and spiritual values of life. For religious rights are the basis for human rights.

The German people were conditioned to hate and be intolerant of the Jewish people before the methodic killing and destruction of human life began. Spiritual freedom and political liberty were not honored or protected. There was apathy toward evil and evil prevailed.

"Good people" lived *in the towns nearby*, but they did not get involved to stop Auschwitz. They did not concern themselves with Dachau or any of the other places of human destruction.

The apathy and non-involvement of the "good people"—the church people—in the Nazi government activities of the 1930s, made it easy not to smell the burning stench of human flesh in the 1940s.

Ignoring the educational process of discrimination in the 1930s, allowed the minds of the "good people"—the church people—to be closed to the realities of torture, murder, and abuse of the 1940s. The surprise of the Hitler era was not that one man could be so evil, but that so many failed to do good.

How could the German people live with all the evidence that would point to the massacre of six million Jews? You wonder - how could it happen? How could people live *in the town nearby* smelling the stench and not do something about it? How could they see the thousands of peoples hauled by trains or marching through their towns never to return and not do something about it? How could they live next door to people who worked in those installations of death without doing something about it?

And yet today, here in America, we see millions of Americans doing nothing about forces mounting in this land to deny us our life, our hopes, and our purpose. What is mankind without political liberty and spiritual freedom?

While it's easy to get indignant about the inhumane, the diabolical actions of Hitler, we in America today are denying life to one and a half million aborted babies each year. Oh, there are a few people who protest—a few people who try to change the law, a few people who march and write letters—but where is the voice of the Christian church? Where is the Jewish community? What are the silent people doing while this destruction of human life is carried out? It is murder—let's call it murder.

Where is the social conscience of America? Where are the people who cherish and hold life so dear? In an historical perspective, we are the ones now living *in the towns nearby* just as those Germans were in the late 1930s and the early 1940s. We are blaming legislators, the Supreme Court, the hospitals. But it is we who have allowed the selfishness of America to demand the destruction of life for the convenience of the moment.

There are other issues in America where we see millions of silent people living *in the towns nearby*—not getting involved, not being committed, not standing for what is right. And yet as those issues continue their march, there is the erosion of our political liberty and spiritual freedom.

We should talk about schools and education. We all believe in education. It is critical to America. And yet the monopolistic public school systems have deteriorated year after year. Too many of our children are almost illiterate—boys and girls are graduating from high schools when they can't read sufficiently well to fill out an application for a job. Too many children have low moral values—school boards do not allow the teaching of right from wrong. We have allowed our classrooms to be taken over in some instances by secular humanists who believe that man and not God is at the center of all things and who do not share the fundamental commitments of America to assure political liberty and spiritual freedom.

What do most Americans do? Most Americans live *in the town nearby* and are too busy to be concerned with those political matters. We don't serve on the school board, nor do we vote in the school board elections. In too many instances, we simply surrender the right to run the schools to those activists who would seek to implement philosophies and programs that bring about the deterioration of our public school systems. Thus our public schools become government schools, weakening political liberty and spiritual freedom.

In the early days of the Republic, public schools were to be encouraged in America because we believed that all people were entitled to an education. The states carried out the responsibilities of seeing that all Americans had an opportunity for an education. And in that frame work, we taught the values of America— we taught patriotism, we encouraged religious commitment. We started the day in many of our schools with the pledge of allegiance to the flag and a prayer to God.

And yet today, through actions of state legislatures, the United States Supreme Court, and the Congress of the United States, the right of the children to have organized voluntary prayer is denied. The fundamental values of religious teachings are denied. The teaching of patriotism that is critical to the survival of a national spirit and the continuation of a strong country is diminishing. And what do the parents of the children do? We live *in a town nearby.* We don't recognize the stench or the marching of the enemy.

Today, America is confronted with yet another controversy that threatens our very existence—the nuclear freeze movement.

The free people of the world do have an enemy—Communism. Many argue that the Communists don't seek to dominate and control the world—they argue that the Communist leaders want peace and can be reasoned with.

The facts are to the contrary. The atheistic forces of Communism proclaim that they will dominate and rule the world. Their relentless march of oppression hammers out their determination.

The spokesmen of the present nuclear freeze movement have failed to review history. In 1939, there was only one Communist country—Russia—accounting for about 7 percent of the earth's population. After the great victory in World War II, Communist forces created the Iron Curtain. Millions of people lost their freedom and liberty to a government of oppression. The hammering march took Albania, Bulgaria, Yugoslavia, Poland, Romania, Czechoslovakia, North Korea, Hungary, East Germany, and Mainland China. All lost to the Communist forces in the late 1940s. Then came the loss of Tibet in 1951, North Vietnam in 1954, and Cuba in 1960. Cambodia, Laos, and South Vietnam in 1975. Afghanistan and Nicaragua in 1979. Add Mozambique, Angola, South Yemen, and Ethiopia to the list. As a result, in 1983 the Communist governments now control more than a third of the world's population.

In spite of these historical facts, respected spokesmen call for a nuclear freeze that would give Communist forces throughout the world a clear advantage.

It is important that those of us who are evangelical and fundamental in our faith take a position on this moral issue and not surrender the political debate to the liberal spokesmen of the religious communities.

I do not intend to argue the merits. The proper conclusion, as seen from my perspective, is very clear. We must champion peace—and peace only comes with strength. We must never allow this great stronghold of spiritual freedom to agree to a freeze of its military capabilities at a level of inferiority.

In the last fifty years, the role of the government in our private lives has escalated in unprecedented dimensions. As the government itself grows stronger, the citizen's participation in that government grows weaker. With less involvement and a more dominating government, the threats to liberty and freedom are much greater.

It is time for renewal. It is time for recommitment. When I was a young boy, the common teaching was that, to be socially acceptable, you didn't speak about religion or politics. That is wrong on both counts. Unfortunately, that is still the way many in America are taught. As a consequence, we have a hurting nation.

Let us come out of our silence. Let us be bold to stand. Let us dare to speak. We need to speak about the Judeo-Christian commitment of this country. We need to talk about our spiritual freedom and our political liberty. We need to get involved.

It is wrong for the Jews and the Christians of America to stay out of political issues. We must get involved if we are to fight for the fundamental freedoms, the fundamental principles, and the fundamental commitments to faith. We must not abandon those principles which are based upon absolutes. There **are** absolutes in this world. And to deny this, is to deny God. Without God, this nation cannot and will not survive, nor does it deserve to.

We must see to it that our people are active in community affairs. We can encourage their involvement by example, from the pulpit, with special committees, through education, with action groups or by other means. But we must be successful in involving moral people in politics and government activities. To live in America means every adult should be responsible for the course of our nation.

We must see that the faithful are involved in the school system. We must see that the faithful are involved in private welfare and charity programs of this nation. We must see to it that the faithful are involved in the total life of a community. The faithful must be active in political activities—not as a church or synagogue, but as individuals who are aware of their spiritual freedom and their political liberty.

If the Christians and Jews are not also active in politics, they will lose that which is critically important to America. My challenge to the Christians and Jews is to get involved—to be involved in politics—to make the decisions that count—and to do whatever is necessary to see to it that there is a balanced perspective as we seek to champion and defend those forces that would guarantee us our liberty and our freedom.

I am not indicating that there will, or should, be a monolithic voice. The strength of

America is the pluralistic society that allows the several divisions in the Protestant Church, the Catholic Church, and the Jewish community. We must even tolerate those who stand against all of the fundamental principles.

The same is true in the political world. Not every Christian will be committed to the same political resolution. But every Christian should be committed to some political resolution. In our democracy, the pluralistic society must be championed and protected. The worst option available to America is non-involvement by the spiritually inclined. For all legislation is based on moral values and moral values should be weighed by the fundamental teachings of the religious perspective.

To pretend that you may not mix religious and political activities is an hypocrisy that can no longer be afforded in this country.

The constitutional provisions were set up so that the state could not dictate the existence of a national church. Its purpose was to protect spiritual freedom and not put the force of government behind any one expression of religious activity. The objective was to protect a pluralistic society. It was never meant to exclude those who follow God. That constitutional principle has been prostituted severely by the enemies of spiritual freedom in an effort to curtail the expression of religious freedom. We must fight and resist in every possible way those forces which seek to limit our spiritual freedom.

My mind shifts back to January of this year, when my wife and I stood hand in hand in the Simon Wiesenthal Holocaust Memorial Center in Los Angeles. We studied the pictures on the walls of that Memorial—pictures that portrayed the unfolding of the history of the hatred and discrimination that swept across Europe in the 1930s leading to the death and destruction of eleven million human beings— six million of them Jews. On one of the walls of the Memorial is a picture of one survivor of a German death camp, pointing with shame at pictures of the world political and religious leaders of the 1930s and 1940s.

Below the picture of the survivor are the words which have been seared in my mind forever:

Here is to the world that did not care— those who had ears but would not hear, those who had eyes but would not see, [those who had mouths but would not speak...].

As I read those words, I renewed my life's commitment to the battle for spiritual freedom and political liberty.

Let it never be said of us that we would not hear, or would not see, or would not speak.

We must courageously defend those principles that are America. No price is too great.

Thank you.

THE WHITE HOUSE
Office of the Press Secretary
(Santa Barbara, California)

For immediate Release   November 26, 1983

RADIO ADDRESS
BY THE PRESIDENT
TO THE NATION

Rancho del Cielo
Santa Barbara, California

9:06 A.M. PST

THE PRESIDENT: My fellow Americans, there's a change of management over at the Department of Interior. James Watt has resigned. And Judge William Clark has taken his place.

When Jim became Secretary of Interior, he told me of the things that needed doing, the things that had to be set straight. He, also, told me that, if and when he did them, he'd probably have to resign in 18 months. Sometimes, the one who straightens out a situation uses up so many brownie points he or she is no longer the best one to carry out the duties of day-to-day management. Jim understood this. But he, also, realized what had to be done. And he did it for more than 30 months, not 18.

Now, with the change in management, it's time to take inventory. The federal government owns some 730 million acres—about one-third of the total land area of the United States. The Department of Interior has jurisdiction over most of that, including our national parks, wildlife refuges, wilderness lands, wetlands, and coastal barriers. Not included in those [370] 730 million acres are our offshore coastal waters—the outer continental shelf, which is, also, Interior's responsibility. And I've asked Bill Clark to review policy, personnel, and process at the Department of the Interior.

Our national parks are the envy of the world. But in 1981, they were a little frayed at the edges. Since 1978, funds for upkeep and restoration had been cut in half. Jim Watt directed a billion dollar improvement and restoration program. This five-year effort is the largest commitment to restoration and improvement of the park system that has ever been made.

You, of course, are aware of the economic crunch we've been facing. Yet, even so, Secretary Watt set out to increase protection for fragile and important conservation lands. In 1982, he proposed that 188 areas along our Gulf and Atlantic coasts be designated as undeveloped coastal areas. And that proposal became the basis for the historic Coastal Barrier Resources Act. This act covers dunes, marshes, and other coastal formations from Maine to Texas—lands that provide irreplaceable feeding and nesting grounds for hundreds of species of water fowl and fish. And, under Secretary Watt, we've added substantial acreage to our parks and wildlife refuges, and some 15,000 acres to our wilderness areas.

Interior is, also, in charge of preserving historic sites and structures. In the Economic Recovery Program we launched in 1981, we gave a 25 percent tax credit for private sector restoration of historic structures. The result has been private investment in historic preservation five times as great as in the preceding four years. Secretary Watt has explored other ways to involve the private sector in historic preservation. And one of the efforts we're all proudest of is the campaign to restore Ellis Island and that grand lady in New York Harbor, the Statue of Liberty. This campaign is being led by Lee Iacocca, the Chairman of Chrysler and is being financed almost entirely by private contributions.

Preservation of endangered species is also a responsibility of the Department. And the approval and review of plans to bring about recovery of endangered plant and animal species has nearly tripled in the 30 months of Secretary Jim Watt. From the very first Jim pledged to the Governors of our 50 states that the Department would be a good neighbor, that they would be included in land planning and that small tracts of isolated federal lands would be made available to communities needing land for hospitals, schools, parks or housing. He also stated that isolated small tracts would be sold to farmers and ranchers.

An example of what I'm talking about is a strip of land one mile long and only two to 20 feet wide that was recently sold. I think you can imagine how these efforts must have erased some problems private landowners had with clouded title to their property.

Of course all this was distorted and led to protests that he was selling national parks and wilderness. What he actually did was sell, in 1982, 55 tracts that totaled only 1,300 acres and this year 228 tracts totaling a little over 10,000 acres. The largest parcel was 640 acres. That's one square mile. None of it was park, wildlife refuge, wilderness or Indian trust lands. They are not for sale. And not one acre of national parkland was leased for oil drilling or mining, contrary to what you may have read or heard.

When territories were becoming states, they were promised title to federal lands within their borders, some lands to be used for public education. But as more and more Western states joined the Union, there began to be a delay. In fact, a permanent delay in turning over these lands. Jim Watt promised the Governors that if they'd identify lands they had a right to claim under their statehood acts, we'd make the federal government honest.

The Governors responded and as a result by the end of this year more land will have been delivered to the states to support their school systems than at any time since 1969.

Changes have been made in the management of forest lands which are eligible for multiple use. Those lands will provide lumber on a sustained-yield basis. This will beneift (sic) Americans who cherish the dream of owning their own home.

We've made giant strides in implementing a national water policy which recognizes state primacy in managing water resources.

People must be a part of our planning and people need a reliable, safe drinking water supply, water for generating power and water for irrigation.

Since I've mentioned energy, let me touch on that for a minute. It's estimated that 85 percent of the fuel we need to keep the wheels of industry turning is on federal (sic) owned property, including the Outer Continental Shelf. Efforts to increase the supply of energy have been carried out in full compliance with environmental stipulations. We can and will have an increased energy supply with an enhanced environment.

James G. Watt has served this nation well. And I'm sure William Clark will do the same.

Until next week, thanks for listening and God bless you.

END   12:11 P.M. PST

PHOTO AND DOCUMENT CREDITS

CPSIA information can be obtained at www.ICGtesting.com
Printed in the USA
LVOW11s0822291113

363030LV00001B/10/P

9 781626 974500